The Music & Movies

of **ELVIS**

By Susan Doll, Ph.D.

Susan Doll holds a Ph.D. in radio, television, and film studies from Northwestern University. An instructor of film studies at Oakton Community College and a writer of film and popular culture, she is an expert on the works and life of Elvis Presley. She has appeared on *The Joan Rivers Show* and National Public Radio to discuss Presley and other topics related to popular film. She is the author of numerous books on popular culture, notably *Elvis: A Tribute to His Life, The Films of Elvis Presley, Marilyn: Her Life and Legend, Elvis: Rock 'n' Roll Legend, Best of Elvis, Understanding Elvis, Elvis: Forever in the Groove, Elvis: American Idol,* and *Florida on Film.*

Acknowledgments

Page 27: Lyric from "Burning Love" copyright ©1972 Sony/ATV Songs LLC. All rights administered by Sony/ATV Music Publishing, 8 Music Square West, Nashville, TN 37203. All rights reserved. Used by permission.

Additional Copyright Information

Walk the Line ©2005 20th Century-Fox Film Corporation, 80; "All Shook Up" single ©BMG/RCA Victor, 6, 16; "Blue Christmas" single ©BMG/RCA Victor, 20; "Burning Love" single 1972 ©BMG/RCA Victor, 26; "Don't Be Cruel" single ©BMG/RCA Victor, 13; "Elvis An American Trilogy" single ©BMG/RCA Victor, 6, 24; "G.I. Blues" single ©BMG/RCA Victor, Contents; "Hound Dog" single ©BMG/RCA Victor, 13; "Suspicious Minds" single ©BMG/RCA Victor, 6, 26; *50,000,000 Elvis Fans Can't Be Wrong* album ©BMG/RCA Victor, 30; *Blue Hawaii* soundtrack ©BMG/RCA Victor, 6, 19, 38; *Elvis: 30 #1 Hits* CD ©BMG/RCA Victor, 46; *Elvis Christmas Album* ©BMG/RCA Victor, 20; *Elvis Is Back!* ©BMG/RCA Victor, 30, 36; *Elvis Presley* album ©BMG/RCA Victor, 30, 34; *From Elvis in Memphis* album ©BMG/RCA Victor, 42; *From Nashville to Memphis: The Essential 60's Masters* box set ©BMG/RCA Victor, 51; *He Touched Me* album ©BMG/RCA Victor, 40; *How Great Thou Art* album ©BMG/RCA Victor, 40; *Jailhouse Rock* soundtrack ©BMG/RCA Victor, 35; *Love Me Tender* soundtrack ©BMG/RCA Victor, 18; *Reconsider Baby* album ©BMG/RCA Victor, 48; *That's the Way It Is* album ©BMG/RCA Victor, Contents, 30, 44; *The King of Rock 'N' Roll: The Complete 50's Masters* box set ©BMG/RCA Victor, 51; *This Is Elvis* album ©BMG/RCA Victor, 68; *Walk a Mile in My Shoes: The Essential 70's Masters* box set ©BMG/RCA Victor, 50; *Heartbreak Hotel,* Buena Vista Pictures, Silver Screen Partners III, Touchstone, 75; *Honeymoon in Vegas,* Castle Rock Entertainment, New Line Cinema, Columbia Pictures, 70, 74; *Elvis* ©1979 Dick Clark Productions, ABC, 70, 72; *Lilo & Stitch* still from the Disney motion picture ©Disney Enterprises, Inc., 70, 78; "Hound Dog" sheet music ©1956 EP Music, 14; *Mystery Train,* JVC Entertainment, Orion Classics, MGM/UA, 76; *It Happened at the World's Fair* ©1963 MGM, 73; *Viva Las Vegas* ©1964 MGM, 64; *Harum Scarum* ©1965 MGM, 66, 67; *Live a Little, Love a Little* movie promotion featuring "A Little Less Conversation" ©1968 MGM, 47; *Elvis on Tour* documentary ©1972 MGM, 69; *G.I. Blues* ©1960 Paramount Pictures Corporation, 58; *Loving You* ©1957 Paramount Pictures Corporation, 56; *Blue Hawaii* ©1961 Paramount Pictures Corporation, 60; "That's All Right" ©Sun Records, 8; "Heartbreak Hotel" sheet music ©1956 Tree Publishing Co., 10; *Follow That Dream* movie poster ©1961 United Artists Corporation, 62.

Photo credits:
Front cover: **PIL Collection.** Back cover: **Dwight K. Irwin** (top); **PIL Collection** (bottom).

Maria Columbus Collection: 9, 23, 27, 39, 43, 47, 52; ©**Corbis:** Bettmann, 12 (top left), Brooks Kraft, 28; **Susan Doll Collection:** 48; **Sharon Fox Collection:** 13 (left), 18, 21, 30 (top right & bottom right), 44, 61, 67, 69, contents (right center & bottom right); **Getty Images:** 25, 37; Michael Ochs Archives, 15; **Globe Photos:** 12 (top right & left center); Bill Hill, 32; NBC, 49; **Dwight K. Irwin:** 4; **Image of Lilo and Stitch from the Disney motion picture** *Lilo & Stitch* ©**Disney Enterprises, Inc.:** 78; **Photofest:** 20th Century-Fox Film Corporation, 80; ABC, 70 (top left), 72; Buena Vista, 75; Columbia Pictures, 70 (bottom), 74; Orion Classics, 76; **PIL Collection:** 6, 8, 10, 13 (right), 14, 16, 19, 20, 22, 24, 26, 40, 42, 46, 50, 51, 66, 68, 70 (top right), 73; MGM, 64; RCA, 30 (top left & bottom left), 34, 35, 36, 38; **Ger Rijff Collection:** contents (bottom left), 54, 56, 58, 59, 62; **Rockin' Robin Rosaaen~All The King's Things Collection:** 45, 60; **Showtime Archives:** Colin Escott, 11; **SuperStock:** Michael Rutherford, 17.

Colorizing: **Cheryl Winser**

Contents

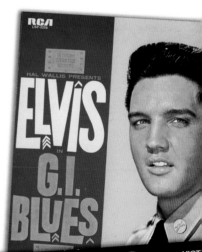

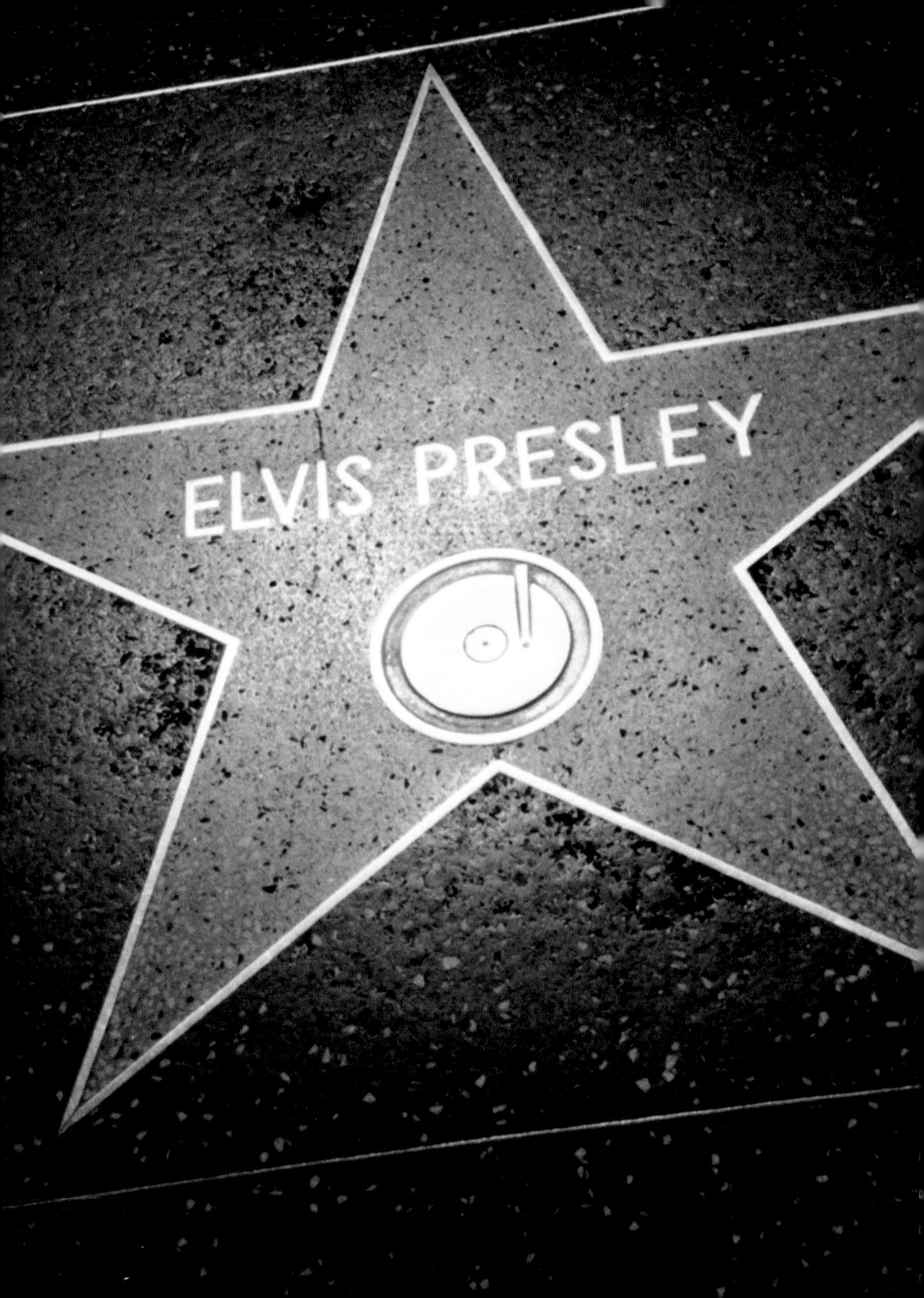
ELVIS PRESLEY

More than a Refresher Course

This book examines some of Elvis's most important music and movies. All the songs, films, and artists have been carefully selected to represent integral parts of his career.

One of the challenges in doing a book about Elvis's work is to offer insights that have not been offered before or give opinions that will help the reader see something familiar in a new light. This book explores famous films and signature songs with new information and reconsiders lesser known movies and tunes in novel ways. For example, songs or films that seem to have little in common on the surface are paired so that a new perspective can be illustrated.

Elvis records for RCA for the first time on January 10, 1956.

Most of Elvis's music and movies are widely available on CD, video, and DVD. So after reading *The Music & Movies of Elvis,* pick out your favorite films and tunes and pair them up in order to re-examine, re-evaluate, and re-interpret them as this book has done. That way you will get a fresh look at someone who truly rocked the world.

Opposite page: *Elvis Presley received his star on the Walk of Fame on Hollywood Boulevard to honor his recording career.*

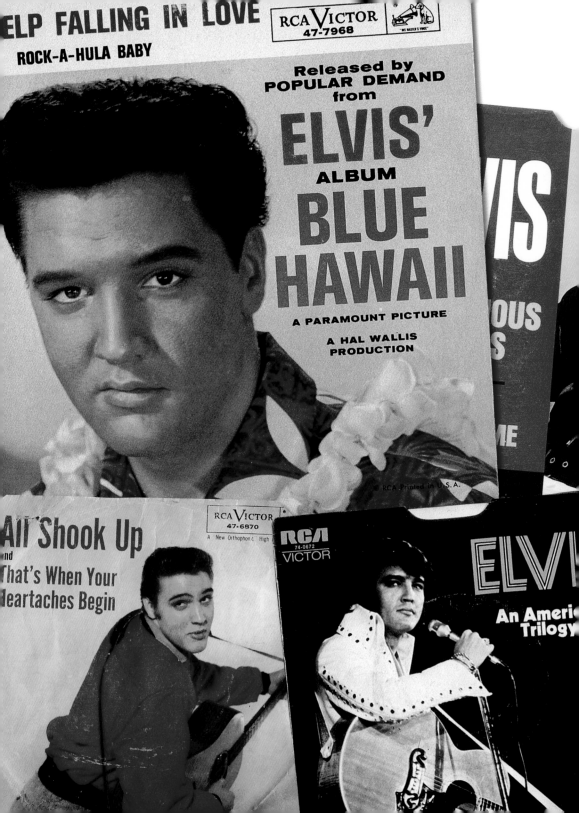

Chapter 1

The Singles

When Elvis began his career, the single record dominated the buying habits of the public. For that reason, Elvis's singles provide a good starting place to examine his music.

In the Beginning

"That's All Right"

Elvis Presley's first single, "That's All Right" backed with "Blue Moon of Kentucky," was released by Sun Records in July 1954. "That's All Right," written and recorded by country blues singer Arthur "Big Boy" Crudup, was considered a standard, conventionally structured blues tune. Meanwhile, "Blue Moon of Kentucky" was a country hit made popular by Bill Monroe, regarded as "the father" of bluegrass music. Elvis's treatment of both songs was far more easygoing than either of the originals, giving his renditions an air of spontaneity.

Elvis's Sun Singles

1. "That's All Right"
   "Blue Moon of Kentucky"

2. "Good Rockin' Tonight"
   "I Don't Care If the Sun
   Don't Shine"

3. "Milkcow Blues Boogie"
   "You're a Heartbreaker"

4. "Baby Let's Play House"
   "I'm Left, You're Right,
   She's Gone"

5. "Mystery Train"
   "I Forgot to Remember
   to Forget"

Elvis replaced the hard vocal delivery and the tense rhythm of "That's All Right" with a relaxed vocal style and rhythm. For "Blue Moon of Kentucky," the tempo was sped up and two elements were added that would make Elvis famous: the syncopation of certain lyrics while he sang and a reverberation during recording, resulting in an echo effect.

Elvis's approach and sound became known as "rockabilly," a term referring to the fusion of country music (commonly called hillbilly music) with rhythm and blues that has been relaxed and sped up, or "rocked." The word rockabilly was not coined until long after Presley was established, suggesting that the industry did not understand the ramifications of his explosive combination of two types of Southern music for a long while.

"Mystery Train"

Of Elvis's five singles for Sun, "That's All Right" and "Blue Moon of Kentucky" generally receive the most critical attention in accounts of Presley's career because they were the first to be released. "Mystery Train," however, is mentioned in passing but rarely thoughtfully explored.

R&B singer Herman "Little Junior" Parker and Sam Phillips wrote "Mystery Train," which was based on an old Carter Family tune titled "Worried Man Blues." Considered the First Family of Country Music, the Carters had built their repertoire from all-but-forgotten Appalachian folk tunes that were rearranged by A. P. Carter. Parker and Phillips gave the Carters' tune a bluesier, mournful tempo and much darker lyrics, turning it into "Mystery Train."

Elvis's spin on Parker's song was to speed it up and emphasize the rhythm. The result is a traditional country song that was reworked as a blues tune, then turned into a rockabilly classic. Many claim that Elvis's music represents a true integration of black rhythm and blues and white country music; if that is so, then this song is a telling point in that evolution.

Elvis and Johnny Cash are backstage at the Grand Ole Opry *on December 21, 1956.*

Other Sun Recording Artists

Johnny Cash
Charlie Feathers
David Houston
Jerry Lee Lewis
Roy Orbison
Carl Perkins
Charlie Rich
Billy Lee Riley
Rufus Thomas
Conway Twitty

"Heartbreak Hotel" Revisited

In January 2006, Sony/BMG (the current owners of RCA) and Elvis Presley Enterprises re-released "Heartbreak Hotel" to commemorate the song's 50th anniversary. Like it had in 1956, the song reached number one on the Billboard charts. More than 4,500 copies were sold during the first week, and sales figures climbed to more than 10,500 over the next three weeks. At the end of the month, Sony/BMG celebrated the success of this reissue with the release of a deluxe box set titled *Elvis #1 Singles*. This limited-edition set included 21 of Elvis's #1 hits on individual CD singles, which were made of black plastic with grooves to mimic the look of the original 45s.

Breaking Big

"Heartbreak Hotel"

"Heartbreak Hotel" was Elvis's first single for RCA Victor under his new contract with that label. Unlike the songs he recorded for Sun, "Heartbreak Hotel" was a new tune written especially for him. The song's lyrics, by writers Mae Axton and Tommy Durden, blues-influenced sound, and dramatic tone were tailored to suit Presley's specific singing and performing style.

The song's description of loneliness and alienation coupled with Presley's emotional rendering were aimed at teenagers. As Paul Simpson declared in *The Rough Guide to Elvis*, Elvis expressed "in two minutes and eight seconds what J. D. Salinger had taken a novel to convey in *The Catcher in the Rye*."

The Million Dollar Quartet

At the end of 1956, Elvis enjoyed his first year as the music industry's hottest success story. On December 4, he dropped by Sun Studio for a friendly visit with Sam Phillips. On that day, Carl Perkins, who was experiencing his own success with "Blue Suede Shoes," was in the studio recording new material. And a recent Phillips discovery, Jerry Lee Lewis, was there to play piano for Perkins to fatten up his sparse sound.

After listening to the playback of Perkins's session, Elvis, Jerry Lee, and Carl began to jam. At some point, another Sun artist, Johnny Cash, dropped by and joined in. Phillips, who had a nose for significant musical events, left the tapes running to capture the moment for posterity. He also called reporter Bob Johnson to hurry over and catch the fun. The following day, Johnson's article was published in the *Memphis Press-Scimitar* under the headline "Million Dollar Quartet."

The famed Million Dollar Quartet (left to right): Jerry Lee Lewis, Carl Perkins, Elvis, and Johnny Cash.

The quartet's choice of music included mostly country and gospel, reflecting the importance of those genres to the style of all four singers. Perkins took the lead only once on "Keeper of the Key," content to play guitar and supply harmony vocals. Lewis can be heard more frequently, often singing in duet with Elvis. Cash's voice is not readily apparent on any of the published tracks, though Johnson and Perkins verified that he joined in on for at least "Blueberry Hill" and "Isle of Golden Dreams." The song most often discussed by music historians is Elvis's rendition of "Don't Be Cruel" in which he imitates Jackie Wilson imitating him.

Elvis chats with comedian Milton Berle (above) and performs his controversial number (left) on The Milton Berle Show.

Controversy

"Hound Dog"

Elvis's highly charged performance of "Hound Dog" on *The Milton Berle Show* caused more controversy than any other performance in his career. On the surface, the tune seems little more than a novelty number, but its blues roots gave it a sexually provocative connotation that Elvis emphasized when he sang it on national television.

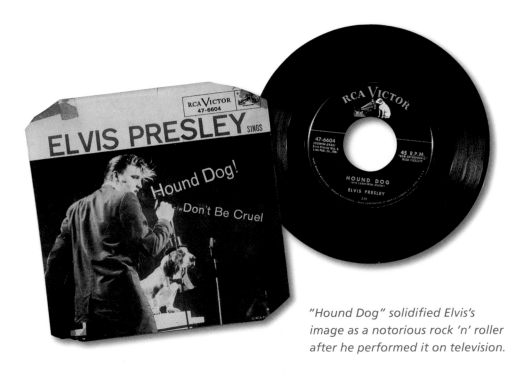

"Hound Dog" solidified Elvis's image as a notorious rock 'n' roller after he performed it on television.

"Hound Dog" was originally written for blues singer Willa Mae "Big Mama" Thornton, who recorded it in 1953. Shortly thereafter, a variety of singers stepped forward to record their own interpretations, including country singer Tommy Duncan, blues singer Little Esther Phillips, and the rock 'n' roll group Freddy Bell and the Bellboys.

Presley preferred Bell's fast-paced rock 'n' roll rendition with the tamer, more obtuse lyrics in which he added the famous line about catching a rabbit. Presley, however, did not record a version of the song until July 2, 1956, almost a month after his notorious performance on Berle's show. He wanted to escape the Sun sound entirely by attempting "something bigger, more explosive." His recording of the song differed slightly from his live television performances, because the tempo is faster and the sound "bigger," perhaps because of the backup vocals by the Jordanaires.

In 1952, Jerry Leiber and Mike Stoller wrote "Hound Dog"—a song about a gigolo—in about ten minutes.

Leiber and Stoller

Too Hip for the Room

During the 1950s boom in popular music, Jerry Leiber and Mike Stoller were among the most highly influential songwriters of the era. Their initial success came as the creators of "Hound Dog" for Big Mama Thornton, which was magnified tenfold after the song was sung by Elvis. Later in the 1950s, particularly through their work with the Coasters and the Drifters, they created a string of groundbreaking hits that are some of the most entertaining in rock 'n' roll history.

During this heady time, they also worked with Elvis on the sound tracks for *Jailhouse Rock* and *King Creole*. In addition to penning the title tracks for both films, they wrote "Love Me," "Treat Me Nice," and "Trouble,"

From left: Stoller, Presley, and Leiber read the sheet music for the film Jailhouse Rock *at the MGM studios in Culver City, California, in 1957.*

among others. The relationship was short-lived in part because Leiber and Stoller refused to put up with Colonel Parker's shenanigans. Nevertheless, the pair was also notorious for growing bored with the artists they worked with and could be insufferably smug in their comments to the press about certain popular performers of the day.

In the 1960s, the pair settled down and started their own record label, Red Bird, to record girl groups. Leiber and Stoller are in the Rock and Roll Hall of Fame, the Songwriters Hall of Fame, and the Record Producers Hall of Fame.

Leiber and Stoller's Biggest Hits

"Hound Dog" (1956)
Elvis Presley, No. 1

"Jailhouse Rock" (1957),
Elvis Presley, No. 1

"Don't" (1958),
Elvis Presley, No. 1

"Yakety Yak" (1958),
The Coasters, No. 1

"Kansas City" (1959),
Wilbert Harrison, No. 1

"Charlie Brown" (1959),
The Coasters, No. 2

"There Goes My Baby" (1959),
The Drifters, No. 2

"Stand by Me" (1961),
Ben E. King, No. 4

"On Broadway" (1963),
The Drifters, No. 9

Otis and Elvis

"All Shook Up"

"All Shook Up" reached #1 on both the U.S. and U.K. Jukebox charts.

Of the thousand or so songs Otis Blackwell wrote during his lifetime, "Don't Be Cruel" is undoubtedly the most widely known. Blackwell's other songs for Elvis, however, are also noteworthy because they not only reveal his diversity as a songwriter but they also spotlight the professional chemistry he shared with Elvis.

Blackwell's inspiration for the title "All Shook Up" allegedly came from a mundane incident straight out of everyday life, though the story has undoubtedly been enhanced over the decades. While working for Shalimar Music as a songwriter, Blackwell was sitting in the office trying to come up with a new powerhouse tune. Al Stanton, one of the partners in the music publishing company, dropped in while downing a bottle of cola. He shook up the bottle so that the contents foamed and fizzled over, casually remarking, "Why don't you write a song about that?" A couple of days later, Blackwell surprised Stanton with a draft of "All Shook Up."

Contrary to some reports, Blackwell did not compose the tune specifically for Elvis as a follow-up to "Don't Be Cruel." Two other singers, David Hill and Vicki Young, recorded "All Shook Up" before him. Elvis recorded the tune in Hollywood at Radio Recorders in January 1957. In his version, Elvis overdubbed himself slapping the back of his guitar, which is a pleasant reminder of his Sun Studio sound.

"Return to Sender"

This nicely penned tune by Blackwell and Winfield Scott is the best part of the film *Girls! Girls! Girls!,* though it almost didn't make it into the film. Blackwell had not yet submitted the song to the producers when he accidentally ran into Colonel Parker at Hill and Range music publishers in New York. Parker persuaded Blackwell to play the song for him and immediately recognized its potential as a hit.

Elvis loved the finely crafted pop song, and his recording of it owes much to the high-energy style of Jackie Wilson, whom he greatly admired. In the film, Elvis even seems to emulate Wilson's performing style when he holds his arms out to his sides, shrugs his shoulders, and snaps his fingers. "Return to Sender" was Elvis's last million-seller for three years and the last big hit written for him by Blackwell. Elvis did record one more Blackwell song titled "One Broken Heart for Sale," but it lacked the spark of the other tunes. Blackwell fell out of favor with Presley's management after his title song for the film *Roustabout* was rejected.

An excellent rock 'n' roll songwriter, Blackwell was influenced by mainstream pop music rather than the regional sounds of country or R&B. His songs added a different flavor to Elvis's repertoire.

A Unique Collectible

On January 8, 1993, the U.S. postal service released a stamp commemorating Elvis Presley. Enterprising stamp collectors put the Elvis stamps on letters that day and mailed them off with fake addresses. That way they would be sent back marked "Return To Sender" and become collectors' items.

Movie Milestones

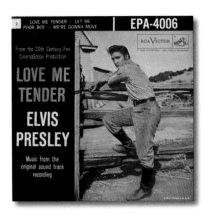

The movie version of "Love Me Tender" had slightly different lyrics and an additional verse than the version on this EP.

Movie Misfire

There are a lot of candidates for the worst song Elvis recorded for a movie, but "Yoga Is as Yoga Does" must be near the top of the list. Part of the *Easy Come, Easy Go* sound track, the tune is supposed to ridicule crazy fads of the 1960s, including yoga, which was not a mainstream lifestyle choice at the time. The lyrics, however, are so poorly conceived, the song succeeds only as a lampoon of Elvis's musicals.

"Love Me Tender"

After his Hollywood career was over, Elvis seldom sang any of the 200-plus songs from his 29 feature films. It was no secret that he was disillusioned with his film career, and this disappointment carried over to the sound track tunes. Two of the exceptions were "Love Me Tender" and "Can't Help Falling in Love," which became a standard part of his concert performances.

"Love Me Tender" was the title song from his first feature film, which was originally called *The Reno Brothers*. When advance sales for "Love Me Tender" exceeded one million copies, the film was retitled to capitalize on the name recognition. The ballad was based on a sentimental, Civil War-era folk song called "Aura Lee," or "Aura Lea," written by George R. Poulton and W. W. Fosdick.

When Elvis returned to live performances during the 1970s, he incorporated "Love Me Tender" into his act as a love song for his fans in the audience. When the opening notes of the song began to play, fans would come down to the front of the stage and "interact" with Elvis. They handed him roses, gifts, or notes, and he gave them kisses and hugs, sometimes re-giving the flowers to other fans. It became a ritual of adulation and appreciation that never diminished with time.

"Can't Help Falling in Love"

Hill and Range, the music publishers associated with RCA, churned out many of the songs for Elvis's films. Their songs for these movies are generally derided for their bland sound and mediocre lyrics. One exception is "Can't Help Falling in Love," which Hill and Range writers Hugo Peretti, Luigi Creatore, and George Weiss turned from an 18th-century French melody titled "Plaisir d'Amour" into a sincere love song

Elvis received his 29th gold record for "Can't Help Falling in Love."

Ironically, Hill and Range originally rejected the song, but Elvis rescued it and suggested it might work for *Blue Hawaii*. The version sung in the film is Elvis's best rendering, because the accompaniment is so slight that the singer's sincere interpretation seems heartfelt and true. The sound track offers a similar but shorter version.

During the concert years of the 1970s, Elvis used "Can't Help Falling in Love" as his final number, often speeding it up to hurry off the stage. Like "Love Me Tender," however, the song was intended as a valentine to the faithful fans who stuck by him to the bitter end.

Christmas with Elvis

Christmas Albums

Elvis' Christmas Album, released in 1957 and reissued in 1964

Elvis' Christmas Album, 1970

Elvis Sings the Wonderful World of Christmas

Memories of Christmas

All-Time Christmas Favorites (possible bootleg)

"Blue Christmas"

"It really is the best season of the year. The Christmas cards, trees and lights just grab you. There is something about Christmas and being home that I just can't explain. Maybe it's being with the family and with friends, time to read and study. And, of course, there are the snowball fights and sleigh rides and yes, just home."

Elvis expressed these heartfelt words about the holidays to his hometown newspaper, the *Memphis Press-Scimitar,* in 1966. His love for the season prompted Elvis to release several Christmas albums and singles during his career, beginning with *Elvis' Christmas Album* in 1957.

It is difficult to imagine "Blue Christmas" as any other singer's song, but this modern-day Christmas tune had been recorded several times prior to Elvis's 1957 version. In 1949, three singers had hits with the song, including Russ Morgan, Hugo Winterhalter, and country legend Ernest Tubb, and the following year, Billy Eckstein recorded a popular version of it. With his deep, soulful voice, Elvis rocked this pop tune and made it his own. Though the song debuted on *Elvis' Christmas Album,* it was released as a single in 1964.

"Merry Christmas Baby"

Elvis recorded this little-known gem during a jam session at RCA's Nashville studios on May 15, 1971, but the song has a long R&B history. Written in 1949 by Lou Baxter and Johnny Moore, "Merry Christmas Baby" was first recorded by Moore's Three Blazers. It reached number nine on Billboard's R&B chart. The song was reissued in 1950 and 1954, though the attribution was changed on the reissues. Other recordings of the song include those by Chuck Berry in 1958 and Dodie Stevens in 1960.

In this wonderfully gaudy Christmas postcard, Parker is dressed as Santa, and Elvis wears the "Burning Love" jumpsuit from 1972.

"Merry Christmas Baby" and "Blue Christmas" make a provocative pairing for a number of reasons. The former is as unknown as the latter is famous; one is down and dirty, and the other is a sad-sack love song. In "Merry Christmas Baby," the singer sarcastically snarls at his former love, while in "Blue Christmas," he laments he is spending the holiday alone.

"Merry Christmas Baby" represents the blues end of Elvis's musical spectrum, a reminder of the regional influences on his style. "Blue Christmas" reveals how Elvis molded his regional influences into a sound palatable to the mainstream public. It is a testament to his talent that he felt at home singing both songs.

Civil Rights

"If I Can Dream"

The NBC-TV special *Elvis,* now called *The '68 Comeback Special,* closed with the moving contemporary spiritual "If I Can Dream." The song was written at the last minute at the request of the show's producer, Steve Binder. The musical director for *Elvis,* W. Earl Brown, wrote the song as a response to the assassinations of Robert Kennedy and Martin Luther King, Jr. It was intended as a statement of hope for the future of America. Elvis loved "If I Can Dream," and he gave it everything he had.

"If I Can Dream" was a heartfelt plea for understanding, reflecting the turbulent times.

The instrumental track was recorded on June 20 or 21, 1968. Elvis sang the song while the instrumental part was being recorded. Though his vocals were not to be used on the final version, he still sang it with the passion the song inspired, even dropping down on his knee at one point. The effect left the string section with their mouths open. Later, he re-recorded the vocals in a darkened studio, and once again, he "performed" the song rather than merely recording it.

"If I Can Dream" climbed to number 12 on the charts and earned Elvis another gold record.

"In the Ghetto"

The first generation of rock 'n' roll critics and reviewers were hard on Elvis Presley, accusing him of selling out in the 1960s by turning away from rock 'n' roll toward pop music and losing himself in the endless series of musical comedies. Some suggest that the politics and social revolution of the era passed him by. "If I Can Dream" and "In the Ghetto" prove otherwise.

Martin Luther King, Jr., had been killed in his hometown of Memphis, which appalled Elvis, because he felt it confirmed everyone's worst fears about the South. When Robert Kennedy was also killed, Elvis was in California working on his television special, and the news unnerved him. Though some of his views were more conservative than the generation that came after him, Presley knew what was going on in his country and he cared about it.

All the King's Men: Elvis's Music Producers

Sam Phillips (1954–1956)

Chet Atkins (1956–1960s)

Felton Jarvis (1966–1977)

Chips Moman (1969)

Record producer Felton Jarvis steered Elvis toward better music during the late 1960s.

Still, when songwriter Mac Davis submitted "In the Ghetto" for Elvis to record, Elvis had reservations about its themes of racism and classism. Some of his entourage suggested he not record it, but when producer Chips Moman asked if he could give the song to someone else, Elvis decided to record it. After he made the decision, the singer became committed to the song, performing it with sensitivity and strength. Elvis's version of the song eloquently but forcefully captures the consequences of an endless cycle of racism and poverty.

23

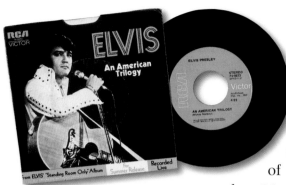

RCA released this single in February 1972.

His Life in Song

The following songs recorded and performed by Elvis are generally considered to be autobiographical, though these assumptions are often exaggerated.

"Memphis, Tennessee"

"Don't Cry Daddy"

"Mama Liked the Roses"

"Good Time Charlie's Got the Blues"

"Hurt"

"Separate Ways"

"You Gave Me a Mountain"

"My Way"

Southern Man

"American Trilogy"

Elvis never lost his identity as a Southerner—a fact born out of his refusal to live anywhere but Memphis. Some of the songs he chose to record and perform in concert reflect his Southern roots and his kinship for his homeland.

"American Trilogy" combines "Dixie," "Battle Hymn of the Republic," and the spiritual "All My Trials" into a medley originally arranged and recorded by country singer Mickey Newbury in 1971.

The song is a microcosm of Southern history in which the Confederate anthem "Dixie" collides with the Union's "Battle Hymn of the Republic," while the quiet strains of "All My Trials" echoes the civil rights movement. The tempos of the songs in this arrangement are not traditional: "Dixie" has been slowed down, resulting in a lonely, wistful quality; "All My Trials" is rendered in a poignant whisper; and "Battle Hymn of the Republic" slowly builds to a powerful crescendo, which provides the climax of the song. The piece conveys the trials and tribulations of the South as a battleground for the Civil War in the 19th century and the civil rights movement in the 20th century through the melancholy strains of "Dixie" and "All My Trials." At the same time, it points to pride and hope in a better future in the powerful crescendo of "Battle Hymn."

Presley's dramatic performance of the medley, in which he bowed his head, dropped to one knee, and spread his cape to resemble a pair of wings, added a passion to the piece that other performers could never have pulled off.

"Polk Salad Annie"

Elvis's version of "Polk Salad Annie" by Southern rocker Tony Joe White was recorded while he performed onstage at the International Hotel in Las Vegas in 1970. Funky, sexy, and low-down, the song was the epitome of swamp rock or a Southern-style rock 'n' roll.

The song was filled with Southern slang and cultural references that must have made mainstream audiences curious.

Tony Joe White in concert, 2003

The title made reference to an herb known in the South as pokeweed, among other names. In the song, the singer declares he wants a "mess of it," meaning he desires a serving of it for a meal.

In addition to "Polk Salad Annie," Elvis recorded two other Southern-flavored compositions by White—"I Got a Thing About You Baby" and "For Ol' Times Sake."

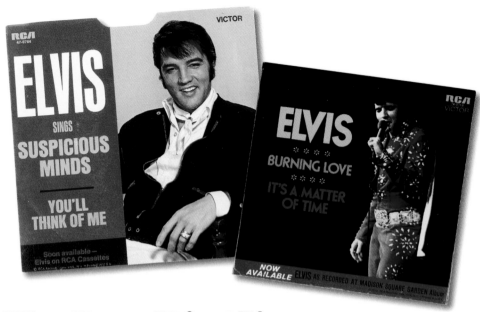

The Last Big Hits

"Suspicious Minds"

Released in late 1969, "Suspicious Minds" proved to be Elvis's last single to reach number one on the Billboard charts. At four minutes and 22 seconds, it was his longest-running number-one song. "Suspicious Minds" was recorded at American Sound Studios in January 1969. Produced by Chips Moman, this fast-paced number with a propulsive bass line blended a thundering sound of horns, strings, and drums along with the voices of Elvis and a choir of female backup singers. As the song reached its climactic moments, all elements were propelled forward at breakneck speed, rising in a seemingly endless crescendo.

The song was even more dramatic in his Las Vegas shows, where he stretched it into a powerhouse showstopping piece, which often ran eight minutes.

"Burning Love"

The highlight of Elvis's studio sessions in Hollywood in March 1972 was the recording of "Burning Love," written by Dennis Linde, who had composed the song especially for Elvis. The song's explosive energy and fast pace make it a timeless rock 'n' roll number, while the phrase "hunka hunka burnin' love" is indelibly linked to Presley. The recording owed a great deal to Elvis's long-time drummer, Ronnie Tutt, whose pounding rhythm drove the song. Linde himself added to the recording, overdubbing a raucous guitar lick on the song's bridge.

Ironically, according to some sources, Elvis did not like the song for reasons no one can quite explain. He had to be convinced to record it, and he sang it as little as possible thereafter. In addition, RCA buried "Burning Love" on an album of old movie tracks that they titled *Burning Love and Hits from His Movies, Vol. 2.* Despite Elvis's reservations and RCA's bad marketing decision, "Burning Love" became a worldwide hit in 1972, peaking at number two on Billboard's Hot 100 chart.

Elvis performs in his Burning Love jumpsuit, occasionally called the "Red Matador," in the fall of 1972.

The Gold and Platinum Singles

- *Heartbreak Hotel / I Was the One,* 2X Platinum
- *Blue Suede Shoes / Tutti Frutti,* Gold
- *I Want You, I Need You, I Love You / My Baby Left Me,* Platinum
- *Hound Dog / Don't Be Cruel,* 4X Platinum
- *Love Me Tender / Any Way You Want Me,* 3X Platinum
- *Too Much / Playing for Keeps,* Platinum
- *All Shook Up / That's When Your Heartaches Begin,* 2X Platinum
- *(Let Me Be Your) Teddy Bear / Loving You,* 2X Platinum
- *Jailhouse Rock / Treat Me Nice,* 2X Platinum

- *Don't / I Beg of You,* Platinum
- *Wear My Ring Around Your Neck / Doncha' Think It's Time,* Platinum
- *Hard Headed Woman / Don't Ask Me Why,* Platinum
- *I Got Stung / One Night,* Platinum
- *(Now and Then There's) A Fool Such as I / I Need Your Love Tonight,* Platinum
- *A Big Hunk o' Love / My Wish Came True,* Gold
- *Stuck on You / Fame and Fortune,* Platinum
- *It's Now or Never / A Mess of Blues,* Platinum
- *Are You Lonesome Tonight / I Gotta Know,* 2X Platinum
- *Surrender / Lonely Man,* Platinum

28

- *I Feel So Bad / Wild in the Country*, Gold
- *(Marie's the Name) His Latest Flame / Little Sister*, Gold
- *Can't Help Falling in Love / Rock-a-Hula Baby*, Platinum
- *Good Luck Charm / Anything That's Part of You*, Platinum
- *She's Not You / Just Tell Her Jim Said Hello*, Gold
- *Return to Sender / Where Do You Come From?* Platinum
- *One Broken Heart For Sale / They Remind Me Too Much of You*, Gold
- *(You're the) Devil in Disguise / Please Don't Drag That String Around*, Gold
- *Bossa Nova Baby / Witchcraft*, Gold
- *Kissin' Cousins / It Hurts Me*, Gold
- *Viva Las Vegas / What'd I Say*, Gold
- *Ain't That Loving You, Baby / Ask Me*, Gold
- *Crying in the Chapel / I Believe in the Man in the Sky*, Platinum
- *I'm Yours / Long Lonely Highway*, Gold
- *Puppet on a String / Wooden Heart*, Gold
- *Blue Christmas / Santa Claus Is Back in Town*, Platinum
- *Tell Me Why / Blue River*, Gold
- *Frankie and Johnny / Please Don't Stop Loving Me*, Gold
- *If I Can Dream / Edge of Reality*, Gold
- *In the Ghetto / Any Day Now*, Platinum
- *Clean Up Your Own Back Yard / The Fair Is Moving On*, Gold
- *Suspicious Minds / You'll Think of Me*, Platinum
- *Don't Cry Daddy / Rubberneckin'*, Platinum
- *Kentucky Rain / My Little Friend*, Gold
- *The Wonder of You / Mama Liked the Roses*, Gold
- *I've Lost You / The Next Step Is Love*, Gold
- *You Don't Have to Say You Love Me / Patch It Up*, Gold
- *I Really Don't Want to Know / There Goes My Everything*, Gold
- *Burning Love / It's a Matter of Time*, Platinum
- *Separate Ways / Always on My Mind*, Gold
- *Way Down / Pledging My Love*, Platinum
- *My Way / America*, Gold
- *That's All Right*, Gold
- *Good Rockin' Tonight*, Gold

Chapter 2

The Albums

By the end of Elvis's career, the long-playing album had replaced the single as the format of choice for the record-buying public. A look at some of his key albums offers insight into his career and the music industry of another era.

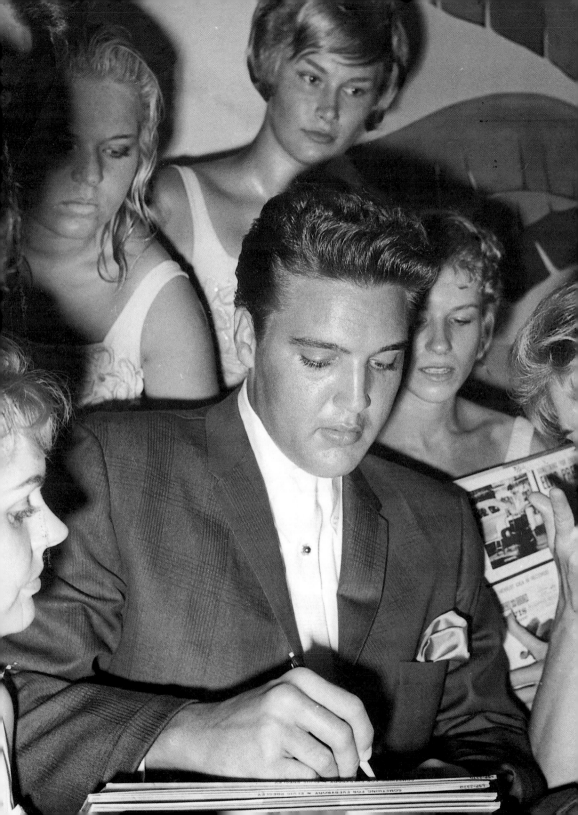

The Presley Albums

Elvis's albums are not the stellar example of music-making one might associate with someone of his historical importance. Several reasons exist for this unexpected situation. During the 1960s, he recorded mostly sound-track albums, and as his films deteriorated in quality, so did the songs. In the 1970s, his touring and Las Vegas appearances so dominated his career that the grind of the road interfered with cutting new material.

In addition, Elvis's management, including the Colonel and the execs at RCA, pressured him to record the songs published by Hill and Range, the music publisher associated with Elvis and the Colonel. Songwriters working for Hill and Range were required to give Elvis a songwriting credit or filter part of their royalties to Elvis Presley Music and Gladys Music, two subsidiaries of Hill and Range that existed to provide Elvis and the Colonel with a cut of the royalties. This arrangement scared away the best songwriters, resulting in a shortage of solid material for Elvis to record. Still, Elvis cut several albums that showcased his unique talents, and these are included in this chapter.

After Elvis's death, RCA recklessly released whatever songs were left in the vault, or they endlessly reissued the same material, drowning Elvis's legacy in a sea of poorly planned albums. In 1986, BMG (later Sony/BMG) purchased RCA, and a new strategy was developed to research and restore the Presley catalogue of recordings. A committee of experts was organized to coordinate Elvis's music, resulting in the release of a number of high-quality compilations of his songs.

Opposite page: Adoring fans watch as
Elvis autographs copies of his new album
Something for Everybody.

Elvis Presley

The First Album

Elvis Presley

"Blue Suede Shoes"

"I'm Counting on You"

"I Got a Woman"

"One-Sided Love Affair"

"I Love You Because"

"Just Because"

"Tutti Frutti"

"Tryin' to Get to You"

"I'm Gonna Sit Right Down and Cry (Over You)"

"I'll Never Let You Go (Little Darlin')"

"Blue Moon"

"Money Honey"

Elvis began work on his first album in Nashville on January 10–11, 1956. Legendary guitarist Chet Atkins, RCA's head supervisor in Nashville at the time, organized the sessions. In addition to Elvis regulars Scotty Moore, Bill Black, and D. J. Fontana, the sessions featured Atkins on rhythm guitar, Floyd Cramer on the piano, and gospel singers Ben and Brock Speer (of the Speer Family) and Gordon Stoker (of the Jordanaires) as background vocalists.

Elvis's unique approach to recording—in which he repeatedly "performed" each song as though singing it for an audience before instinctively selecting the best take—unnerved the RCA execs. The sessions, however, yielded several great tracks, including "Heartbreak Hotel," "Money Honey," and a cover of Ray Charles's "I Got a Woman." A second session in New York yielded additional cuts. Seven tracks from the two sessions were chosen for the album, along with five songs previously recorded at Sun but never released. The song selection for the album, combined with the musicians who worked the sessions, reveals that the heart of Elvis's style was still his ability to fuse diverse musical influences, including pop, R&B, and country. The LP *Elvis Presley* was released by RCA Victor on March 13, 1956, and sold 360,000 albums by the end of April. A two-record EP featuring 8 of the LP's 12 songs was released on the same day.

What's an EP?

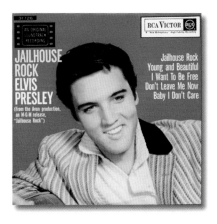

An extended-play album, or EP, is a vinyl record or CD that contains more than one single but is too short to qualify as a long-playing album, or LP. Typically, an LP has eight or more tracks (25–80 minutes), a single has one to three (5–15 minutes), and an EP has four to seven (15–25 minutes).

The Best of Elvis's EPs

EPs have been released in various sizes in different eras. In the 1950s and 1960s, EPs were typically 45 RPM recordings on 7-inch disks, with two songs on each side. By coincidence, the format gained popularity just as Elvis became a national recording sensation, and during that time, he dominated Billboard's EP charts, hitting number one six times and making the top ten 16 times. According to the Elvis Presley

Elvis Presley (three-record set, October 1956)

Jailhouse Rock (1957)

Peace in the Valley (1957)

King Creole, Volumes I and II (1958)

See the USA, the Elvis Way (1964)

Estate's official Web site, Presley's EPs earned six gold, eight platinum, and two multi-platinum RIAA certifications, representing sales of more than 16.5 million units.

Though not as popular as EPs were in Elvis's day, they are still a part of the recording industry.

Elvis Is Back!

Released in April 1960, *Elvis Is Back!* was the singer's first LP after his discharge from the army the month before. Though critics and skeptics assumed Elvis's two-year absence from the pop music scene would severely hurt his popularity, *Elvis Is Back!* did moderately well. The album appeared on Billboard's LP charts for 56 weeks, peaking at number two.

Songs for *Elvis Is Back!* were recorded at Nashville's RCA studios in March and April, with Chet Atkins in the control booth once again. Nashville's A-list of studio musicians, including Floyd Cramer, Boots Randolph, Hank Garland, Bobby Moore, and Buddy Harmon, were tapped to back Elvis, along with Scotty Moore and D. J. Fontana.

Like his earlier work, this album offers an eclectic collection of musical genres, from a sentimental duet with friend Charlie Hodges called "I Will Be Home Again" to the pop stylings of "Fever" to the provocative "Such a Night." In retrospect, the album represents a peak in the singer's career, when his maturity and confidence led to a control and focus in his music.

Chet Atkins

Country music's premiere guitarist, Chester Burton Atkins was born on June 20, 1924, in Luttrell, Tennessee. Quiet, intelligent, and intuitive, Atkins enjoyed dual careers in the music industry. To the public, he was the legendary guitarist who had recorded several successful

Chet Atkins (far left) leads Elvis through a recording session in 1956.

instrumental records and albums. To industry insiders, he was one of RCA's best musicians and production supervisors, who arranged and played on musical sessions for the label's artists. In that capacity, he helped create the Nashville Sound—a smooth style of country music that owed as much to pop as it did to honky tonk.

Atkins not only helped supervise the 1956 recording sessions that resulted in Presley's first album, but he also backed him on rhythm guitar. Atkins's participation was a dream come true for Scotty Moore, who greatly admired the accomplished guitarist. In 1960, Atkins was promoted to A&R (artist and repertoire) manager. He pulled together Nashville's best sessions musicians to play on *Elvis Is Back!* and supervised the proceedings. In 1968, he became vice president of RCA's country division. Atkins died in 2001.

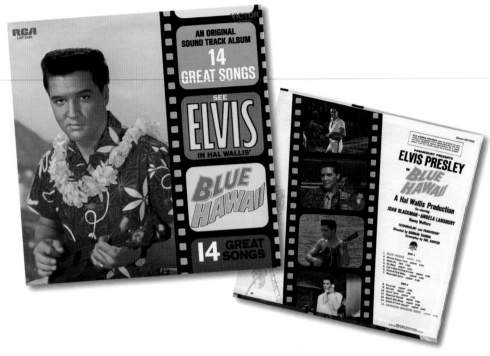

Blue Hawaii

The sound track to *Blue Hawaii* became Elvis's biggest-selling sound-track album, reaching number one on Billboard's LP charts two months after its release in October 1961. It was the number-one LP in America for five months and remained on the album charts for 79 weeks. According to the Recording Industry Association of America (RIAA), it has attained triple platinum status (as of 2007).

Blue Hawaii features 14 songs, the most of any sound track for a Presley film. The tunes are solid examples of the blend of pop and rock that defined Elvis's movie music in the 1960s. Some of the songs were not written for the film but were selected because of their Hawaiian themes, including "Moonlight Swim," "Blue Hawaii," and "Hawaiian

According to The Rough Guide to Elvis, *the only LP to sell more copies than* Blue Hawaii *in the 1960s was* West Side Story.

Blue Hawaii

"Blue Hawaii"

"Almost Always True"

"Aloha Oe"

"No More"

"Can't Help Falling in Love"

"Rock-a-Hula Baby"

"Moonlight Swim"

"Ku-u-i-po"

"Ito Eats"

"Slicin' Sand"

"Hawaiian Sunset"

"Beach Boy Blues"

"Island of Love (Kauai)"

"Hawaiian Wedding Song"

Wedding Song." "Aloha Oe" was actually composed by Queen Liliuokalani of Hawaii in 1878 and recorded by Bing Crosby in the 1930s during a craze for all things tropical. To capture the Hawaiian-style sound, special musicians were employed for the recording sessions, including percussionist Hal Blaine, who was an expert in Hawaiian instruments, and ukelele and steel guitar players.

Sing Me Back Home: Elvis and Gospel Music

Peace in the Valley and His Hand in Mine

While Elvis recorded gospel music throughout his singing career, the Grammy Award-winning LP *How Great Thou Art* (1967) may be Elvis's most well-known gospel effort. Although he had eclectic tastes and gave any kind of music a fair listen, Elvis loved and sought solace in gospel music.

Peace in the Valley, an EP released in March 1957, was Elvis's first major religious recording and the best-selling gospel EP of all time. *Peace in the Valley* featured four songs, but the title tune was the reason for the EP's existence. Written by Rev. Thomas A. Dorsey in 1939, "Peace in the Valley" was a gospel classic that Elvis had sung on his third appearance on *The Ed Sullivan Show* and dedicated to the relief workers for a Hungarian earthquake disaster.

His Hand in Mine (1960) was Elvis's first long-playing gospel album. The most powerful track was Elvis's rendition of "Mansion Over the Hilltop," a 1949 song by Ira Stanphill in which the "mansion" of the title is a metaphor for heaven. *His Hand in Mine* sold well and spent 20 weeks on Billboard's LP chart. By 2007, it had achieved platinum status.

He Touched Me

Released in April 1972, *He Touched Me* featured 12 inspirational songs. Some of the songs were classics, such as "Amazing Grace," but others were contemporary compositions. Andrae Crouch wrote "I've Got Confidence," and Jerry Reed composed "A Thing Called Love." Elvis also invoked the style of the male gospel quartets he loved with "Bosom of Abraham" and "I John," while drawing upon black gospel for "I've Got Confidence." *He Touched Me* charted for only ten weeks and never climbed higher than #79 on Billboard's album listing. It won a Grammy, however, and eventually achieved platinum status (by 2007).

In accounts of his career, Elvis's gospel recordings often take a backseat to his innovative rock 'n' roll music of the 1950s and his concert music of the 1970s, but he was an excellent enough gospel performer to be inducted into the Gospel Hall of Fame in 2001. Gospel music was the one constant into Elvis's life. It was the music he first sang as a child; it inspired him to pursue a musical path; it had always calmed his nerves before a recording session or performance; and it was performed at his funeral. As they say in the South, it called him back home.

Grammy Awards

Elvis won only three Grammys during his lifetime—all of them for gospel recordings. The album *How Great Thou Art* won Best Sacred Performance in 1967, the album *He Touched Me* won Best Inspirational Performance in 1972, and a live version of the song "How Great Thou Art" won Best Inspirational Performance in 1974.

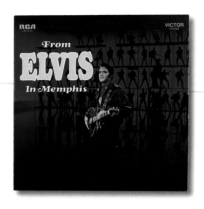

From Elvis in Memphis

Coming Home

Elvis returned to his hometown of Memphis in January 1969 to record *From Elvis in Memphis* and parts of the double album *From Memphis to Vegas/ From Vegas to Memphis* at American Sound Studios. A successful independent recording studio, American Sound was operated and co-owned by Chips Moman, who produced an amazing run of 97 chart records during this time. In addition to *From Elvis in Memphis* and sides three and four of *From Memphis to Vegas/From Vegas to Memphis,* Moman produced several top twenty singles for Presley, including "In the Ghetto," "Kentucky Rain," "Suspicious Minds," and "Don't Cry Daddy."

These Memphis sessions represented Elvis's official break from the pop-rock idiom associated with his movies. Aside from "Love Me Tender," "Jailhouse Rock," and "Can't Help Falling in Love," Elvis would rarely sing any of the 200-plus tunes from his movie career during his concert years.

From Elvis in Memphis

"Wearin' That Loved on Look"

"Only the Strong Survive"

"I'll Hold You in My Heart"

"Long Black Limousine"

"It Keeps Right on a-Hurtin'"

"I'm Movin' On"

"Power of My Love"

"Gentle on My Mind"

"After Loving You"

"True Love Travels on a Gravel Road"

"Any Day Now"

"In the Ghetto"

"The Fair Is Moving On"

"Suspicious Minds"

"You'll Think of Me"

"Don't Cry Daddy"

"Kentucky Rain"

"Mama Liked the Roses"

Moman and his American Sound Studios influenced Elvis's style via the house band, which consisted of a generation of white Southern musicians who had themselves been inspired by Elvis in the 1950s. Presley had personal connections with some of these band members, including guitarist Reggie Young and organist Bobby Emmons, who had played with Bill Black's Combo after Black had struck out on his own, and drummer Gene Chrisman, whom Presley had known from

Jerry Lee Lewis's band. These musicians were younger than the session musicians at RCA's recording facilities in Nashville as well as more attuned to a black blues/rhythm and blues sound. Their style of music, which has been referred to as blue-eyed soul or swamp pop, was distinctly Southern in flavor and yielded a significant influence on Elvis's 1970s style and song choices.

The songs in these albums ranged from contemporary soul ("Only the Strong Survive") to country tunes ("From a Jack to a King"). Some of the original compositions had been penned by country music songwriters such as Jer-

From left: Bobby Wood, Mike Leech, Tommy Cogbill, Gene Chrisman, Elvis, Bobby Emmons, Reggie Young, Ed Kollis, and Dan Penn.

ry Reed, Mac Davis, and Eddie Rabbitt, who had also been influenced by Elvis's 1950s style. Though seemingly diverse in style, the songs Elvis recorded were unified by their arrangements. The resulting sound would be amplified to an epic scale for Elvis's concert performances by an accompaniment that included a country rock band, an orchestra, a male gospel quartet called the Imperials (later replaced by J. D. Sumner and the Stamps), and the Sweet Inspirations backup trio.

That's the Way It Is

Heartsongs

That's the Way It Is

"I Just Can't Help Believin'"

"Twenty Days and Twenty Nights"

"How the Web Was Woven"

"Patch It Up"

"Mary in the Morning"

"You Don't Have to Say You Love Me"

"You've Lost that Lovin' Feeling"

"I've Lost You"

"Just Pretend"

"Stranger in the Crowd"

"The Next Stop Is Love"

"Bridge Over Troubled Water"

Despite the title, this album is not the sound track from the 1970 documentary. Only two of the tracks, "You Don't Have to Say You Love Me" and "The Next Stop Is Love" were taken from the documentary's sound track. Of the remaining ten songs, four were recorded live at the International and six were recorded at RCA's studios in Nashville.

Most of the songs on *That's the Way It Is* are about love, and they reveal that one of Elvis's strengths as a mature singer was his ability to capture the various moods of love—the joy, the pain, and the loss.

B. J. Thomas had a modest hit with the breezy "I Just Can't Help Believin'" in 1970, but Elvis sang this love song with such a smooth, intimate touch that he made it his own. Other tunes on the album offer a musical meditation on the darker side of love, including "How the Web Was Woven" and "You've Lost that Lovin' Feeling." He also interpreted Paul Simon's "Bridge Over Troubled Water" in a plaintive style, in which the lyrics resonate with pain and loss, leaving Simon to remark, "It was a bit dramatic but how the hell am I supposed to compete with that."

Missed Opportunities

Often lost amidst the large-scale sound, the onstage antics, and the pageantry of his concert years is the fact that Elvis was a passionate ballad singer and a sincere chronicler of love and loss. In 1970, when *That's the Way It Is* was released, all five of his gold singles were ballads. The following year, when Elvis's focus was a below-par country album, there were no gold singles. *That's the Way It Is* may have been the last album that thoroughly explored that aspect of his 1970s music. Beginning in 1971, the Colonel and RCA had difficulty coming up with decent material to record because of their insistence on controlling publishing rights, and most of Elvis's albums were reduced to a hodgepodge of leftover tracks, b-sides, and the occasional new song. Though Elvis recorded some good songs in the 1970s and was an exciting performer in concert for most of that period, the albums lacked consistency and coherency.

Elvis was a dramatic interpreter of ballads and love songs.

45

Elvis: 30 #1 Hits

"Heartbreak Hotel"

"Don't Be Cruel"

"Hound Dog"

"Love Me Tender"

"Too Much"

"All Shook Up"

"(Let Me Be Your) Teddy Bear"

"Jailhouse Rock"

"Don't"

"Hard Headed Woman"

"One Night"

"(Now and Then There's)
A Fool Such as I"

"A Big Hunk o' Love"

"Stuck on You"

"It's Now or Never"

"Are You Lonesome Tonight?"

"Wooden Heart"

"Surrender"

"(Marie's the Name) His Latest
Flame"

"Can't Help Falling in Love"

"Good Luck Charm"

"She's Not You"

"Return to Sender"

"(You're the) Devil in Disguise"

"Crying in the Chapel"

"In the Ghetto"

"Suspicious Minds"

"The Wonder of You"

"Burning Love"

"Way Down"

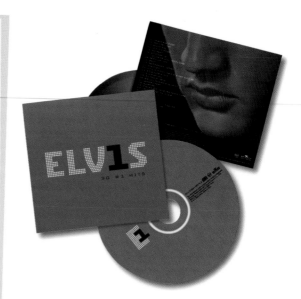

The King Is Dead But Still Selling Albums

Elvis: 30 #1 Hits

Although Elvis Presley died in 1977, his name, music, and image still capture the public's attention. The period after his death has been marked by controversy, acclaim, ridicule, and commercialism. From the pits of tabloid headlines to the peaks of awards and honors, Elvis continues to make news. Death was not the end of Elvis Presley's career; it simply marked another phase.

To commemorate Elvis on the 25th anniversary of his death, RCA released a collection of his number-one songs titled *Elvis: 30 #1 Hits*. The marketing campaign was designed around the tag line: "Before anyone did anything, Elvis did everything." The line succinctly summarized Elvis's contribution to pop culture history while evoking the dynamism of his sound and the danger of his original music. Marketing strategy aside, it was the music that accounted for the album's success. Arranged in chronological order, the collection of hits covered Elvis's entire career at RCA—from "Heartbreak Hotel" in 1956 to "Way Down" in 1977. All the songs reached number one on the charts at the time of their original release, either in the United States or the United Kingdom.

Elvis: 30 #1 Hits rocketed to number one when it debuted, selling 500,000 copies in its first week of release. Debuting an album in the top spot on the U.S. charts was an accomplishment Elvis had not managed while he was alive.

"A Little Less Conversation"

As a last-minute addition to *Elvis: 30 #1 Hits*, the producers included a remix of "A Little Less Conversation," a song Elvis originally recorded for the sound track of *Live a Little, Love a Little*. The song was reworked in early 2002 by a Dutch deejay act called Junkie XL for a Nike World Cup commercial and then released as a dance-mix single. It became Elvis's first top ten single in decades. "A Little Less Conversation" was billed as a bonus track, keeping it separate in concept from the rest of the cuts on the album.

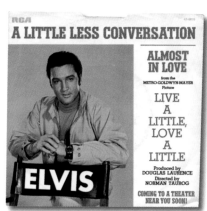

"A Little Less Conversation," released on September 15, 1968, was written by Billy Strange and Mac Davis.

Elvis Sings the Blues

Reconsider Baby

Throughout his career, Elvis recorded the occasional blues song, even during the 1960s when he released mostly movie sound tracks in a slick pop-rock musical style. In 1960, for example, he recorded the insipid "Big Boots" for the sound track to *G.I. Blues,* but he also recorded Lowell Fulson's down and dirty "Reconsider Baby," accompanied by Boots Randolph's sexy-sounding sax. In 1966, he released the ridiculous "Yoga Is as Yoga Does" from *Easy Come, Easy Go,* but he also cut a raw-sounding "Down in the Alley." Released in 1985, *Reconsider Baby* offers a selection of the bluesier tunes Elvis recorded between 1955 and 1971, reminding the world that the roots of his style, even at its most mainstream, came from the indigenous music of the South.

Some of the songs on *Reconsider Baby* are not the versions originally released, adding a freshness to the collection. The album's version of "One Night" was an alternate take, and it featured the original lyrics as sung by Smiley

Lewis ("One night of sin..."). "Ain't That Loving You Baby" was also an alternate take, while "Merry Christmas Baby" was an alternate edit, and "Stranger in My Own Home Town" represented an alternate mix.

"One Night"

Dave Bartholomew and Pearl King wrote the original version of this song in 1956, which was recorded by New Orleans blues singer Smiley Lewis. On January 24, 1957, Elvis did his own version of the song, vbut the lyrics were considered too risqué for his teenage audiences, especially considering the controversy he was still riding out over his provocative performance on *The Milton Berle Show* the previous June. A month later, on February 23, 1957, Elvis recorded a variation in which the singer exclaims to his love that he is praying he can spend one night with her. Though this was considered a cleaned-up interpretation, the lyrics are still suggestive. "One Night" was released on the flip side of "I Got Stung" in October 1958, and it became a top ten hit on Billboard's R&B chart.

Though Elvis came close to singing the original risqué lyrics on *The '68 Comeback Special*, "One Night" was not released until 1983 when it appeared on the LP *Elvis—A Legendary Performer, Volume 4*. Two years later, it was included on *Reconsider Baby*.

Elvis sang "One Night" on The '68 Comeback Special.

The King's Legacy:
The Masters Series

Walk a Mile in My Shoes: The Essential 70s Masters

When BMG purchased RCA, they formed an international committee of record executives to clean up the Presley catalogue. Interested in presenting Elvis's musical legacy, the committee embarked on a long-term goal of restoring and reissuing the music as close to its original form as possible.

Of the three Masters series, *Walk a Mile in My Shoes* is arguably the most thought-provoking because it dispels the negative stereotype of a garish Elvis in his white jumpsuit belting out the same Vegas-style tunes over and over. Instead, this five-disk retrospective of Elvis's work in the 1970s shows how productive the singer was in that decade. Elvis's output during this time may not have been released in well-assembled albums, but the 120 songs in this series reveal an all-around entertainer of eclectic tastes who could master most musical genres.

The Complete 50s Masters and
The Essential 60s Masters I

Released in 1992, *Elvis, the King of Rock 'n' Roll: The Complete 50s Masters* represents BMG's first significant restoration effort. Producers Ernst Jorgensen and Roger Semon searched the RCA vaults from Nashville to Indianapolis to Hollywood to find what they needed for this retrospective of Elvis's complete 1950s output. The five-disk, 140-song set features all of Elvis's released recordings from that era as well as alternate takes and rare live performances. Since its release, *Elvis, the King of Rock 'n' Roll* has gone double platinum, but more importantly, it offers the listener an opportunity to experience the development of Elvis's sound.

Elvis Presley: From Nashville to Memphis: The Essential 60s Masters I is a five-disk, 130-track set that bears witness to the singer's mature, confident pop stylings of the 1960s. The collection begins with Elvis's first sessions after his army discharge and concludes with his historic sessions at American Sound Studios. It does not include the Hollywood movie sound tracks, which were released on a later compilation titled *The Essential 60s Masters II.*

Each Masters series included a booklet written by a respected music historian who put Elvis's music in context.

The Gold and Platinum Albums

- *Elvis Presley,* Gold
- *Elvis,* Gold
- *Loving You,* Gold
- *Elvis' Christmas Album (1957 Package),* 3X Platinum
- *King Creole,* Gold
- *Elvis' Golden Records, Vol. 1,* 6X Platinum
- *50,000,000 Elvis Fans Can't Be Wrong,* Platinum
- *Elvis Is Back!* Gold
- *G.I. Blues,* Platinum
- *His Hand in Mine,* Platinum
- *Something for Everybody,* Gold
- *Blue Hawaii,* 3X Platinum
- *Girls! Girls! Girls!,* Gold
- *Elvis' Golden Records, Vol. 3,* Platinum
- *Roustabout,* Gold
- *Girl Happy,* Gold
- *How Great Thou Art,* 2X Platinum
- *Elvis, NBC-TV Special,* Platinum
- *Elvis' Gold Records, Vol. 4,* Gold
- *Elvis Sings Flaming Star,* Platinum
- *From Elvis in Memphis,* Gold
- *Elvis: From Memphis to Vegas/From Vegas to Memphis,* Gold
- *On Stage, February 1970,* Platinum
- *Worldwide 50 Gold Award Hits,* 2X Platinum
- *Elvis' Christmas Album (1970 Package),* 9X Platinum
- *Elvis, That's the Way It Is,* Gold
- *Elvis in Person at the International Hotel,* Gold
- *Elvis Country,* Gold
- *Elvis: The Other Sides: 50 Gold Award Hits, Vol. 2,* Gold
- *You'll Never Walk Alone,* 3X Platinum
- *Elvis Sings the Wonderful World of Christmas,* 3X Platinum
- *Elvis Now,* Gold
- *He Touched Me,* Platinum
- *Elvis As Recorded at Madison Square Garden,* 3X Platinum
- *Elvis Sings Burning Love and Hits from His Movies, Vol. 2,* 2X Platinum
- *Separate Ways,* Platinum
- *Aloha from Hawaii,* 5X Platinum
- *Elvis, A Legendary Performer, Vol. 1,* 2X Platinum
- *Elvis Recorded Live on Stage in Memphis,* Gold
- *Pure Gold,* 2X Platinum

Opposite page: *The Hall of Gold, part of the Trophy Room at Graceland, showcases Elvis's gold and platinum records.*

- *Elvis, A Legendary Performer, Vol. 2,* 2X Platinum
- *From Elvis Presley Boulevard, Memphis, Tennessee,* Gold
- *Welcome to My World,* Platinum
- *Moody Blue,* 2X Platinum
- *Elvis in Concert,* 3X Platinum
- *He Walks Beside Me,* Gold
- *Elvis, A Legendary Performer, Vol. 3,* Gold
- *Our Memories of Elvis,* Gold
- *This Is Elvis,* Gold
- *Elvis Aron Presley,* Platinum
- *Memories of Christmas,* Gold
- *The Number One Hits,* 3X Platinum
- *The Top Ten Hits,* 4X Platinum
- *Elvis, The King of Rock 'n' Roll, The Complete 50s Masters,* 2X Platinum
- *Elvis, From Nashville to Memphis, The Essential 60s Masters I,* Platinum
- *Elvis: His Greatest Hits (Readers Digest compilation),* Platinum
- *Blue Christmas,* Gold

- *Elvis' Golden Records, Vol. 5,* Gold
- *Amazing Grace,* 2X Platinum
- *If Everyday Was Like Christmas,* Platinum
- *Walk a Mile in My Shoes, The Essential 70s Masters,* Gold
- *50 Years—50 Hits,* 2X Platinum
- *Let's Be Friends,* Platinum
- *Worldwide Gold Award Hits, Vol. 1 & 2,* Platinum
- *The Elvis Presley Story,* 2X Platinum
- *Elvis Gospel Treasury,* Gold
- *The Complete Sun Sessions,* Gold
- *Heart and Soul,* Gold
- *It's Christmas Time,* 2X Platinum
- *The Rock 'n' Roll Era,* Gold
- *The Legend Lives On,* Gold
- *Platinum—A Life In Music,* Gold
- *Elvis 30 #1 Hits,* 4X Platinum
- *Elvis 2nd to None,* Platinum
- *Elvis Sings Hits from His Movies, Vol. 1,* Platinum
- *Almost In Love,* Platinum

- *Double Dynamite,* Platinum
- *Love Me Tender (1987 compilation),* Gold
- *I Got Lucky,* Gold
- *C'mon Everybody,* Gold
- *Frankie and Johnny,* Platinum

Extended Plays

- *Elvis Presley (including "Blue Suede Shoes"),* Gold
- *Heartbreak Hotel,* Gold
- *Elvis Presley (including "Shake, Rattle & Roll"),* Gold
- *The Real Elvis,* Platinum
- *Elvis, Vol. 1,* 2X Platinum
- *Love Me Tender,* Platinum
- *Elvis, Vol. 2,* Gold
- *Peace in the Valley,* Platinum
- *Loving You, Vol. 1,* Gold
- *Loving You, Vol. 2,* Platinum
- *Jailhouse Rock,* 2X Platinum
- *Elvis Sings Christmas Songs,* Platinum
- *King Creole, Vol. 1,* Platinum
- *King Creole, Vol. 2,* Platinum
- *Follow That Dream,* Platinum

Chapter 3

The Movies

This chapter plucks out a handful of movies from Elvis's career as a way to examine his work as an actor. Most represent his best work; a few reveal the downward direction his films took in the mid-1960s. Rather than bemoaning Elvis's failure to make his mark as a major actor, it is more interesting to investigate his career as a movie star.

In Loving You (1957), Jana Lund is about to give Elvis his first onscreen kiss.

Loving You

Pre-Army Rebel

In *Loving You*, Elvis stars as Deke Rivers, a truck driver with a natural singing talent. He teams up with press agent Glenda Markle, played by Lizabeth Scott, in the hopes of becoming the next singing sensation. Glenda takes advantage of his sensual appeal by providing him with custom-ized costumes and arranging publicity stunts, though some of her stunts prove controversial. Any similarity between Elvis's career and the character of Deke Rivers was entirely intentional.

Love Me Tender may have been Elvis's first film, but *Loving You* was the first vehicle to be tailored for his talents and image. In the 1950s, Elvis Pres-ley was considered a notorious rock 'n' roller. *Loving You* capitalized on that image, while at the same time "tam-ing" it. Because Elvis was maligned in the press as a figure of controversy and rebellion, those in charge of his career took on the task of remolding that im-age. By telling parts of his life story

Cast & Credits

Deke Rivers .... Elvis Presley
Glenda Markle .... Lizabeth Scott
Walter Warner .... Wendell Corey
Susan Jessup .... Dolores Hart
Daisy Bricker .... Jana Lund
Sally .... Yvonne Lime
Eddie (bass player) .... Bill Black
Drummer................... D. J. Fontana
Guitar Player.............. Scotty Moore
Bit .... Barbara Hearn
Released by Paramount Pictures on July 30, 1957.
Produced by Hal B. Wallis.
Directed by Hal Kanter.
Screenplay by Herbert Baker and Hal Kanter.
Photographed in VistaVision and Technicolor by Charles Lang, Jr.
Music by Walter Scharf.
Vocal accompaniment by The Jordanaires.

through the familiar form of the Hollywood rise-to-success tale, the producers wanted older viewers to understand that the singer was not all that different from entertainers of the past.

Spotlight on Hal Kanter

To ensure that the film captured the essence of Elvis's life as a performer, producer Hal Wallis sent director/co-scriptwriter Hal Kanter to observe the singer's live appearance on *Louisiana Hayride* on December 16, 1956. Kanter followed Elvis around for a few days in Memphis and then in Shreveport, Louisiana, where *Hayride* was broadcast. Kanter fashioned a script that captured the chaos and exhilaration surrounding Elvis's live performances.

Songs

"Got a Lot o' Livin' to Do"

"(Let's Have a) Party"

"(Let Me Be Your) Teddy Bear"

"Hot Dog"

"Lonesome Cowboy"

"Mean Woman Blues"

"Loving You"

"Dancing on a Dare" sung by Hart's character

"Detour" sung by Hart's character

"The Yellow Rose" sung by Hart's character

"Candy Kisses" performed by the Rough Ridin' Ramblers

The director also worked a "price of fame" theme into the storyline of *Loving You,* suggested by scenes in which fans severely compromise Deke's privacy. In one scene, fans scrawl messages on Deke's car in lipstick, which recalled the times fans had ruined the finish on Elvis's vehicles by leaving love notes in lipstick and nail polish.

The most obvious similarity between the real-life Elvis and the fictional Deke was the controversy both generated due to their performing styles. The film explains that the controversy surrounding Deke is based on a misunderstanding involving miscalculated publicity stunts. By proposing that fictional Deke is merely misunderstood, Kanter implies that Elvis was also misunderstood.

G.I. Blues

Leading Man

Cast & Credits

Tulsa MacLean .... Elvis Presley

Lili .... Juliet Prowse

Cookey .... Robert Ivers

Tina .... Leticia Roman

Rick .... James Douglas

Marla .... Sigrid Maier

Turk .... Jeremy Slate

Musicians .... Scotty Moore
& D. J. Fontana

Released by Paramount Pictures
on November 30, 1960.

Produced by Hal B. Wallis.

Directed by Norman Taurog.

Screenplay by Edmund Beloin and
Henry Garson.

Photographed in Technicolor by
Loyal Griggs.

Music by Joseph J. Lilley.

Vocal accompaniment by
The Jordanaires.

In his first musical comedy, Elvis stars as lady-killer Tulsa MacLean, an army sergeant stationed in West Germany. At the urging of his pals, Tulsa accepts a bet to win the hand of cold-hearted Lili, a beautiful cabaret performer at the Club Europa, played by dancer Juliet Prowse. Just as Tulsa realizes that he is in love with Lili, she finds out that she has been the target of a wager.

G.I. Blues marked the debut of the new Elvis Presley. Taking advantage of the good publicity Elvis received for serving his tour of duty in the army, the Colonel launched a new, more clean-cut image for Elvis after his discharge. Gone were the sideburns the press had found offensive and gone was the flashy, hip clothing. In their place was a more conservative look, one befitting Hollywood's latest leading man. Elvis's music changed as well. Even though some of the songs in *G.I. Blues* were fast-paced, they lacked the hard-driving sound, emotional delivery, and sexual connotations of his pre-army recordings. "Trouble"—the gritty, blues-driven song from *King Creole* in which

Elvis demanded that anyone looking for trouble look into his face—had given way to "Pocketful of Rainbows."

Spotlight on Hal Wallis

G.I. Blues was the third Elvis film produced by Hal Wallis, a respected veteran of the film industry who knew how to groom an actor's image to his best advantage. He had worked in Hollywood since the silent era and would continue to work through the 1970s. Wallis began as a publicity man for Warner Bros. and worked his way up to production head by 1933. There he produced several classics, including *Little Caesar, Sergeant York,* and *The Maltese Falcon.* In 1944, he became an independent producer, releasing his films through Paramount and later Universal. As an independent, Wallis had a reputation for fostering new talent.

In 1964, Wallis produced *Becket*, a high-profile Oscar-winning film, by using his Elvis franchise as collateral. According to some of his friends, Elvis felt used and disillusioned by this point. He had hoped to become a dramatic actor, and he grew to dislike the frivolous musical comedies Wallis and Colonel Parker foisted on him.

Elvis and producer Hal Wallis in the early 1960s. Elvis was under contract to Wallis for a decade and made nine films for him.

Songs

"What's She Really Like"

"G.I. Blues"

"Doin' the Best I Can"

"Frankfort Special"

"Shoppin' Around"

"Tonight Is So Right for Love"

"Wooden Heart"

"Pocketful of Rainbows"

"Big Boots"

"Didja Ever"

Blue Hawaii

The Dye Is Cast

Chad and Maile (Elvis and Joan Blackman) marry in a Hawaiian-like ceremony at the end of Blue Hawaii (1961).

Cast & Credits

Chad Gates................... Elvis Presley
Maile Duval............. Joan Blackman
Sarah Lee Gates... Angela Lansbury
Abigail Prentice .... Nancy Walters
Fred Gates.............. Roland Winters
Mr. Chapman .... Howard McNear
Waihila.......................... Hilo Hattie
Released by Paramount Pictures
on November 22, 1961.
Produced by Hal B. Wallis.
Directed by Norman Taurog.
Screenplay by Hal Kanter.
Photographed in Technicolor and
Panavision by Charles Lang, Jr.
Music by Joseph J. Lilley.
Vocal accompaniment by
The Jordanaires.

Blue Hawaii became the most successful film of Elvis Presley's career. Elvis stars as Chad Gates, whose wealthy family owns a successful pineapple plantation in Hawaii. Chad has just returned from the army at the beginning of the film, and his family is eager for him to pursue the family business. Instead, Chad lands a job as a guide in the tourist agency where girlfriend Maile, played by Joan Blackman, also works.

Blue Hawaii's success sealed Elvis's fate in terms of his film career. Though his earlier attempts to stretch as an actor in the western *Flaming Star* and the drama *Wild in the Country* had not lost money, they had not set the box office afire either. The Colonel used the box-office grosses of *Blue Hawaii* to convince Elvis that his fans preferred him in musical comedies. *G.I. Blues* had introduced audiences to Elvis as the clean-cut leading man, but *Blue Hawaii* typecast him as a leading man of musical comedies, much to his dismay. Despite Elvis's dislike for this film, it is a well-crafted musical that fans remember fondly almost 50 years after it was made.

Spotlight on Hawaii

Much of *Blue Hawaii* was filmed in Hawaii, which had recently joined the union in 1959. The new state was enjoying a high media profile, and the entertainment industry had already taken advantage of the public's interest with the release of *Gidget Goes Hawaiian* and the TV series *Hawaiian Eye*.

The exotic locale was a key element in the promotion of *Blue Hawaii*. It provided more than just beautiful cinematography of Waikiki Beach, Ala Moana Park, Lydgate Park, and the Coco Palms Resort Hotel; it was the perfect setting for romance, and it represented an escape for viewers from the mundane everyday world. Promotion for *Blue Hawaii* promised: "Exciting Romance… Music in the World's Lushest Paradise of Song" and "Elvis Presley Guides You Through a Paradise of Song!"

Exotic settings—and the romance and escape that went with them—became essential ingredients in Elvis's films. Elvis returned to Hawaii to make *Girls! Girls! Girls!* and *Paradise, Hawaiian Style*. Hawaii, Florida, Acapulco, and other vacation locales became such a well-known element in Elvis's movies that he dubbed them "Presley travelogues."

This lei was given to fan clubs as a promotional gimmick for Blue Hawaii.

Songs

"Blue Hawaii"

"Almost Always True"

"Aloha Oe"

"No More"

"Can't Help Falling in Love"

"Rock-a-Hula Baby"

"Moonlight Swim"

"Ku-u-i-Po"

"Ito Eats"

"Slicin' Sand"

"Hawaiian Sunset"

"Beach Boy Blues"

"Island of Love (Kauai)"

"Hawaiian Wedding Song"

Songs

"What a Wonderful Life"
"I'm Not the Marrying Kind"
"Sound Advice"
"On Top of Old Smokey"
"Follow That Dream"
"Angel"

Cast & Credits

Toby Kwimper .... Elvis Presley
Pop Kwimper ...... Arthur O'Connell
Holly Jones .... Anne Helm
Alicia Claypoole .... Joanna Moore
Judge Wardman .... Roland Winters
Nick .... Simon Oakland
George Binkley ..... Howard McNear
Bank Guard .... Red West
Released by United Artists on
May 23, 1962.
Produced by David Weisbart.
Directed by Gordon Douglas.
Screenplay by Charles Lederer.
Photographed by Leo Tover.

Follow That Dream

An Overlooked Gem

In a deviation from his usual musical comedy character, Elvis stars as Toby Kwimper, a L'il Abner-type in a family of simple rural Southerners. The Kwimpers, consisting of Pop, Toby, and several adopted orphans, claim squatter's rights along an unopened stretch of Florida highway. Then they open a small business renting fishing equipment.

Follow That Dream offers a good comeback to anyone who sneers that Elvis's films are all the same. *Dream* does feature Elvis singing six songs, and it is a comedy, but its basis in a satirical novel

by Richard Powell titled *Pioneer Go Home* makes it a unique entry in the Presley filmography. While Powell's novel consists of a sharper satire and a more complex storyline than the film, the screenplay by veteran Hollywood writer Charles Lederer retained some of the novel's witty jabs at modern life.

Spotlight on the Kwimpers

In *Follow That Dream*, the Kwimpers represent the down-to-earth values of rural life, which at first seem outdated and unsophisticated. As the story unfolds, however, viewers realize they have misjudged them, just as the characters in the film do. The Kwimpers may be simple, but they are unaffected by consumerism, free from the pressure of the rat race, compassionate toward the less fortunate, and motivated by the simple pleasures of family, fun, and fishing.

The modern world intrudes upon the Kwimpers via psychologist Alicia Claypoole, two big-city thugs, and a low-level bureaucrat assigned to keep Florida's newest highway in top condition. But they are no match for the Kwimpers. When the humorless bureaucrat discovers Pop Kwimper has accepted numerous government benefits and tries to use that against him, Pop insists that his receipt of relief, disability, and child support stem from patriotism. If the government is so determined to give their money away, then it's his duty as a good citizen to take it from them!

The Kwimpers foil efforts to oust them from their land. In the process, they start their own fishing business and live a life unencumbered by the false values of the modern world. As Toby explains at the end, "I thought there was maybe more to living than the way Pop taught me, but I was never dumb enough to go against him…I was glad I didn't."

Ann-Margret and Elvis enjoyed riding motorcycles both on and off the screen, much to the dismay of the movie's insurance company. In this behind-the-scenes photo, padding is visible in the lower right corner to protect the stars in case of a nasty spill.

Cast & Credits

Lucky Jackson .... Elvis Presley
Rusty Martin .... Ann-Margret
Count Elmo Mancini............. Cesare Danova
Mr. Martin.......... William Demarest
Shorty Farnsworth......... Nicky Blair
Released by Metro-Goldwyn-Mayer on June 17, 1964.
Produced by Jack Cummings and George Sidney.
Directed by George Sidney.
Screenplay by Sally Benson.
Photographed in Metrocolor by Joseph Biroc.
Music by George Stoll.
Choreography by David Winters.

Viva Las Vegas

The Female Elvis Presley

In *Viva Las Vegas,* Elvis was teamed with a costar whose singing and dancing finally matched the intensity of his own performing style. As Rusty Martin, dynamic Ann-Margret perfectly complemented Elvis's character of Lucky Jackson. Lucky, a race-car driver whose car is in desperate need of a new engine, arrives in Las Vegas for the Vegas Grand Prix. He and fellow driver Count Elmo Mancini, played by Cesare Danova, are rivals not only on the track but off the track as well as they compete for the affections of Rusty.

Elvis was not restricted to working only for Hal Wallis and Paramount because the contract he signed with them was not an exclusive one. Elvis worked for other producers at other studios as well, including MGM, United Artists, and Allied Artists. Interestingly, the producers from these other studios tended to follow the musical comedy formula that Wallis had developed for Elvis, occasionally even improving on it. Though *Viva Las Vegas* follows the familiar formula of the "Presley travelogue," the inclusion of dynamic Ann-Margret made it a cut above the rest. Shot predominantly in Las Vegas, the film made effective use of such locations as the Flamingo and Tropicana Hotels and the drag strip at Henderson, Nevada. Meanwhile, songs such as the title song, "What'd I Say," and "C'mon Everybody" enlivened the sound track.

Songs

"Viva Las Vegas"

"The Yellow Rose of Texas"

"The Lady Loves Me"

"C'mon Everybody"

"Today, Tomorrow and Forever"

"What'd I Say"

"Santa Lucia"

"If You Think I Don't Love You"

"I Need Somebody to Lean On"

"My Rival" sung by Ann-Margret's character

"Appreciation" sung by Ann-Margret's character

"The Climb" sung by the Forte Four

Spotlight on Romance

Viva Las Vegas is perhaps best remembered for the romance between Elvis and Ann-Margret. The romance was played out on the front pages of the newspapers after the two were spotted on the town together in Las Vegas. The publicity surrounding the romance was a dream come true for the producers of the film. Ultimately, the romance between these two high-profile stars did not survive the production of the film. Though their relationship did not work, Elvis and Ann-Margret remained friends for the rest of his life. According to Ann-Margret, Elvis sent her flowers in the shape of a guitar on the opening night of every one of her Las Vegas engagements.

Elvis, as Johnny Tyronne, sings to the slave girls of Sinan, Lord of the Assassins.

Harum Scarum

The King Meets the King of the Quickies

A "quickie" produced on a very low budget by Sam Katzman, *Harum Scarum* features Elvis as matinee idol Johnny Tyronne. A take-off on Elvis himself, Johnny is a famous movie and recording star who makes the women swoon and the men jealous. On a personal appearance tour in Lunarkand—a fictional country somewhere in the Middle East—a gang of assassins kidnap Johnny. He escapes and joins a band of pickpockets and rogues, all the while rescuing damsels in distress and singing a variety of pop-styled tunes.

With only an 18-day shooting schedule, *Harum Scarum* was a no-frills production with little time or money to spend on props, costumes, or set design. The temple set had originally been built in 1925 for a Cecil B. DeMille silent feature called *King of Kings*. The costumes worn by the extras in *Harum Scarum* had been used in the 1944 version of *Kismet* and then retailored for the 1955

Cast & Credits

Johnny Tyronne .... Elvis Presley

Princess Shalimar .... Mary Ann Mobley

Aishah .... Fran Jeffries

Prince Dragna .... Michael Ansara

Zacha .... Jay Novello

Baba .... Billy Barty

Distributed by MGM and released on November 24, 1965.

Produced by Sam Katzman.

Directed by Gene Nelson.

Screenplay by Gerald Drayson Adams.

Photographed in Metrocolor by Fred H. Jackman.

Music by Fred Karger.

Vocal accompaniment by The Jordanaires.

musical remake. Even the dagger carried by Elvis had been used in an earlier adventure film, *Lady of the Tropics*. Little effort was invested in the script as well; in fact, the plot was thrown together following the same Presley formula. How bad was it? Well, the Colonel suggested adding a talking camel to the storyline, though the idea was quickly tossed aside.

Spotlight on Sam Katzman

Katzman entered the film industry at the tender age of 13 when he started as a prop boy. Eventually he worked his way up through various studio positions to become a producer. His reputation for producing low-budget films is so prevalent that he has been nicknamed "the King of the Quickies." In his prime, he aimed particularly at the action and juvenile markets. Some of his productions have stood the test of time, including *Rock Around the Clock* and *Your Cheatin' Heart*. The Colonel's decision to team with Katzman signaled a decline in quality for Elvis's films. After this point, the Colonel chose film deals with low budgets and minimum ambition as a way to maximize profits.

Elvis plays Johnny Tyronne, who is in costume as the star of the movie-within-the-movie, Sands of the Desert.

Songs

"Harem Holiday"

"My Desert Serenade"

"Go East, Young Man"

"Mirage"

"Kismet"

"Shake That Tambourine"

"Hey, Little Girl"

"Golden Coins"

"So Close, Yet So Far (from Paradise)"

This Is Elvis

Produced, directed, and written by Andrew Solt and Malcolm Leo, *This Is Elvis* combined news footage, television performances, and re-created scenes with actors to tell the story of Elvis's life and career. The film opens with the shocking news of the singer's death, then flashes back to his childhood in Tupelo, Mississippi, where his story begins. This 1980 docudrama was released three years after Presley's death, when the mainstream media were obsessed with the details of his drug-related death. In focusing on the breadth of his career, his humanity, and most of all his music, the film reminded the public of his accomplishments.

The Documentaries

Elvis—That's the Way It Is

Some claim that the best movies featuring Elvis Presley are documentaries, not narrative films. And, as decades pass and memories fade, these documentaries not only chronicle his music and performing style but also remind younger generations of his impact on audiences.

Elvis's 32nd film, *Elvis—That's the Way It Is,* documented his 1970 summer appearance at the International in Las Vegas. Elvis began rehearsals July 5 at the MGM studios in Hollywood, where he worked on his material for about a month. The show opened August 10. The MGM cameras not only recorded the rehearsals but also opening night, several performances throughout the engagement, and one show at Veterans Memorial Coliseum in Phoenix, Arizona. The film is structured so that the rehearsals and other scenes of preparation build to an extended climax of Elvis onstage. Dressed in a simple, white jumpsuit, accented with fringe instead of rhinestones and gems, Elvis is showcased at the pinnacle of his career.

Elvis on Tour

Elvis on Tour—the second documentary on Elvis—chronicled the singer's extensive 15-city tour in the spring of 1972. Filmmakers Pierre Adidge and Robert Abel succeeded in capturing the hectic pace of Elvis's touring schedule through a montage sequence of the cities he visited.

Costing $600,000, to produce (not counting Elvis's fee of $1 million), *Elvis on Tour* recouped its production costs after three days in the theaters. Documentaries are rarely major box-office draws, but this film was a financial success. Critically acclaimed as well, *Elvis on Tour* won a Golden Globe for Best Documentary. Much

Despite the hard-driving concert tunes, onstage excitement, and flashy jumpsuits, Elvis on Tour *also showcased gospel music in Elvis's act.*

of the creative success of the film was due to its effective editing style, which relied on a split-screen technique to convey the excitement of Elvis in concert. Multiple images of Elvis performing were shown on the screen simultaneously, a technique that had been used in *Woodstock*. The series of scenes from Elvis's movies plus the succession of clips of the different cities visited on the tour also depended on precise editing for its visual impact. In charge of these montage sequences was a young filmmaker named Martin Scorsese.

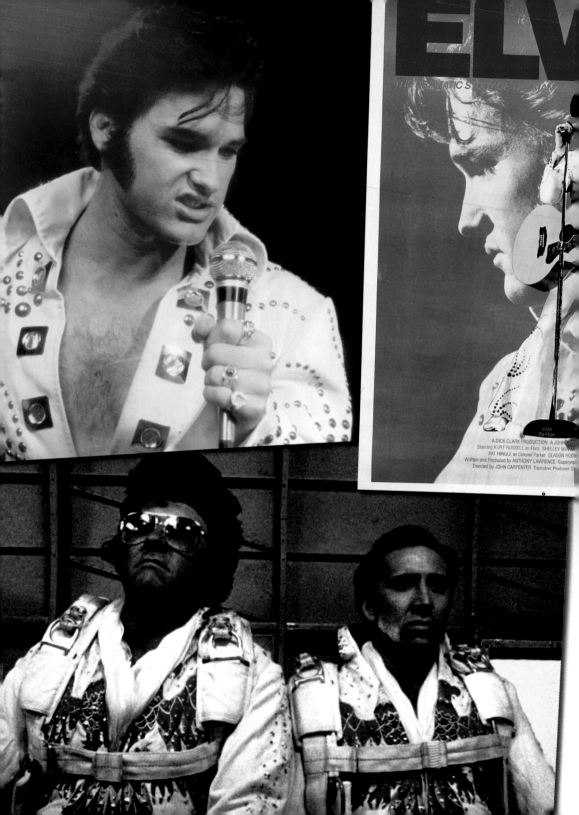

ELV

THE ... STORY OF THE MAN ...

ELVIS
The Movie

A DICK CLARK PRODUCTION A JOHNSON
Starring KURT RUSSELL as Elvis SHELLEY WINTERS
PAT HINGLE as Colonel Parker SEASON HUBL
Written and Produced by ANTHONY LAWRENCE Supervisi
Directed by JOHN CARPENTER Executive Producer Di

Chapter 4

Symbol

Beginning in 1979, a spate of miniseries and made-for-television projects rolled out, all claiming to offer a true slice of Elvis's real life. They range in quality from the thoughtful *Elvis* to the ridiculous *Elvis and the Beauty Queen*. Several movies serve up fictionalized Elvis characters who act as potent symbols, icons, or metaphors in the story. This is part of Elvis's second life—not as a man but as an icon who lives on in songs, art work, tacky souvenirs, television, and, of course, the movies.

Elvis on the Small Screen

Made for Television

Kurt Russell stars as Elvis in John Carpenter's biopic. The role proved Russell's range as an actor, while the movie offered a serious take on Elvis and his music.

On February 11, 1979, ABC-TV aired *Elvis,* the first biographical picture, or biopic, about the singer's life. John Carpenter, a respected moviemaker best known for his horror movies (*Halloween* and *Escape from New York*) directed this well-crafted and sincere made-for-television feature. Dick Clark, a high-profile supporter of rock 'n' roll music since his *American Bandstand* hit the airwaves in 1956, produced it. Airing 18 months after Presley's death, the biopic starred Kurt Russell, who offered a complex, sympathetic portrayal of Elvis during a time when controversy, scandal, and rumor swirled around his drug use and excessive lifestyle.

The success of *Elvis* launched a number of TV biopics over the next 30 years that never surpassed this early effort. *Elvis and the Beauty Queen* (1981), a syrupy account of the relationship between Elvis and Linda Thompson, suffered from the miscasting of Don Johnson, whose raspy tenor voice was the opposite of Elvis's deep low tones.

Some of the TV biopics were adapted from biographies, including *Elvis and Me* (1988), a two-part miniseries based on Priscilla Presley's autobiography of the same title. Dale Midkiff made for a distant, uncharismatic Elvis, though that did not stop 32 million viewers from making it the highest-rated miniseries of the 1988 season.

Elvis and the Colonel (1993), starring the unknown Rob Youngblood as Elvis and Beau Bridges as Colonel Parker, has the same title as Dirk Vellenga's biography of Parker, but its fictionalized account is little more than a simplistic warning about the high price of fame. In 2005, a new biopic titled *Elvis* was fully supported by the Presley estate and became the first to feature Elvis's master recordings. Starring Irish actor Jonathan Rhys Meyers, the two-part miniseries lacked sufficient insight to be anything more than a conventional biopic.

The Series

In the spring of 1990, ABC-TV launched *Elvis,* a television series based on the beginning of the singer's career, before he became a national sensation. The series was short-lived, but it offered the public a thought-provoking interpretation of Elvis's life. Some episodes in the series were allegories that foretold Elvis's eventual impact on popular music and his legendary status as the King of Rock 'n' Roll, while others commented on the effect of his childhood on the rest of his life. *Elvis* the series remains the best interpretation of Presley's life and career because it reached beyond biography to find a deeper meaning.

Kurt Russell

Every few years, actor Kurt Russell takes on a role related to Elvis Presley. The most distinguished example was his Emmy-nominated performance in *Elvis,* but Russell's career connection to Elvis goes back to childhood. In *It Happened at the World's Fair* (1963), ten-year-old Kurt had a walk-on as a bratty boy who kicks Elvis in the shins—a moment captured forever in a famous movie still. In 1994, Russell supplied the voice for the character Elvis Presley in *Forrest Gump.* Onscreen, Peter Dobson appeared as the young Presley, but it was Russell's voice that the viewer heard. In 2001, Russell and Kevin Costner costarred as a pair of Elvis impersonators who are also thieves in *3000 Miles to Graceland.*

Nicolas Cage finds himself as one of the Flying Elvises in Honeymoon in Vegas.

3000 Miles to Graceland

In *3000 Miles to Graceland* (2001), five Elvis impersonators rob a Vegas casino, but plans go awry when the head of the gang betrays his companions. In dressing the thieves like grubby impersonators, who are in effect faux representations of a unique, authentic entertainer, the movie suggests that a corruption of sorts has infested America. Here, Vegas is a dark, gritty town, and the seedy-looking impersonators with their extra-long sideburns and ultra-tacky jumpsuits are more than excessive; they are decadent and vulgar. The twist is that two of them may be Elvis's illegitimate sons, who struggle with their identity. Despite this thoughtful use of Elvis's image as a cultural icon, the poorly crafted movie alienates the audience with nonstop profanity and extreme violence.

Vegas Elvis

Honeymoon in Vegas

The Elvis Presley of the 1970s—with his long sideburns, white jumpsuits, and flashy sunglasses—is often dubbed the "Vegas Elvis." To some, Vegas Elvis is negatively associated with Presley's strange and excessive lifestyle, as though the gaudiness of the costuming is a metaphor for the King's unrestrained appetite for food, drugs, women, and guns. Most impersonators imitate Vegas Elvis, further adding to the negative connotation of this phase of his career. The fact that Elvis experienced some of the finest moments of his career during this era is overshadowed by the stereotype of "Vegas Elvis."

In *Honeymoon in Vegas* (1992), Nicolas Cage plays a marriage-phobic man who agrees to wed his long-suffering fiancee, played by Sarah Jessica Parker, if they tie the knot in Vegas. While there, Parker is put off by the city's surreal atmosphere, emphasized by the legion of Elvis impersonators who populate the background. The recurring joke culminates with the Flying Elvises, a group of 34 impersonators who skydive onto the Vegas Strip as part of their act. The Elvis impersonators are used to show that Vegas is bizarre and completely alien to Parker, who misses her normal life as a schoolteacher.

Original and engaging, *Honeymoon in Vegas* boasts a sound track of Elvis's best tunes, but the film paints the impersonators as farcical, indirectly and unfairly suggesting that Elvis's Vegas era was akin to a circus act.

Heartbreak Hotel

Heartbreak Hotel (1988) offers a portrait of the Vegas Elvis that alludes to the pitfalls of his celebrity. Set in 1972, this warm-hearted comedy involves a teenage boy who kidnaps Elvis and brings him home to his single mother in a small Ohio town. The family has its share of problems. The mother is depressed and lonely, and she always falls for the wrong men; the son lacks self-confidence; and the daughter is afraid

David Keith doesn't look like Elvis, but his Southern accent was solid.

of the monsters that lurk in the dark. Like a bona fide movie hero, Elvis "rescues" them from their problems. As he repairs the fixtures on the house, mows the lawn, and even redecorates, he restores order within the family, fixing broken hearts and mending egos. At the same time, Elvis finds happiness in living an everyday life—something he never does as the King of Rock 'n' Roll. Yet, an air of melancholy hangs over the conclusion when Elvis returns to his world, because the audience knows the eventual outcome of that decision.

Elvis the Icon

Cinque Lee (left) and singer Screaming Jay Hawkins (a contemporary of Elvis's) play the bellhop and desk clerk in Mystery Train.

Other Elvis-Influenced Movies

Touched by Love (1980)

Eat the Peach (1986)

Leningrad Cowboys Go America (1989)

Wild at Heart (1990)

True Romance (1993)

The Woman Who Loved Elvis (1993)

Elvis Meets Nixon (1997)

Finding Graceland (1998)

Elvis Has Left the Building (2004)

Mystery Train

Mystery Train, a unique movie directed by independent moviemaker Jim Jarmusch, tells three seemingly unrelated stories. In the first, a young Japanese couple hooked on American pop culture pass through Memphis as part of their vacation; then an Italian widow on a layover spends the night in a rundown Memphis hotel as she waits for the body of her dead husband to be sent home; finally, a trio of hapless thieves hole up in the same hotel while on the lam. At the end, the viewer discovers that the three stories are happening simultaneously, though the characters have little connection to each other. They remain isolated at the end of their experiences, the victims of the dislocation and alienation that pervade the movie.

The title, which is derived from one of Elvis's Sun recordings, plus the Memphis setting, set the viewer up to expect a movie about Elvis Presley. Yet, Elvis, Graceland, and a recognizable Memphis are noticeably absent. Instead, tacky portraits of Elvis grace the rooms of the cheap, rundown Arcade

Hotel where most of the action takes place; the hotel employees talk about Elvis trivia; guests admire their T-shirts from Graceland; "Blue Moon" plays on the radio in the background; and the confused ghost of Elvis appears briefly in one scene. Like the characters in the movie, the viewer experiences Elvis only as an icon of American pop culture.

To Jarmusch, Elvis has become an icon of a commercialized pop culture that is served up as a substitute for experience, compounding the isolation and alienation of modern society.

Forrest Gump

Forrest Gump (1994) tells the story of a simpleton's epic journey through life in the latter half of the 20th century. Along the way, he encounters real-life historical figures and participates in actual historical events. The movie's special effects team won an Oscar for the computer-generated imagery (CGI) that made it possible for Tom Hanks as Forrest Gump to interact with historical figures in documentary news footage.

One of Forrest's earliest encounters is with a young Elvis Presley in the mid-1950s; however, Elvis is not re-created with CGI but played by actor Peter Dobson and voiced by Kurt Russell. It seems Elvis is a struggling singer staying at the Gump's boarding house and has not yet stumbled onto his signature performing style.

As a child, Forrest wears leg braces because of a spinal condition, so he walks and moves in an awkward, jerky gate. Elvis plays guitar and sings for Forrest, who begins to dance with herky-jerky movements. Inspired by Forrest, Elvis works these movements into his act, and the rest is history. The idea that the most famous entertainer of the 20th century "borrowed" his unique performing style from such humble origins is quaint at best, but ultimately it robs Elvis's style of its sexual undertones and of its cultural significance as a fusion of black and white roots music—two factors that changed the course of popular music.

Animated Elvis

Lilo and Stitch

An animated movie is the perfect vehicle to introduce Elvis Presley to younger generations. In 2001, Disney released *Lilo and Stitch*, using traditional hand-drawn animation that gave the movie a colorful, fanciful look missing from today's 3-D animated features. Set in Kauai, Hawaii, the backgrounds of the Hawaiian setting were akin to watercolor paintings filled with rich, saturated tones. The music of Elvis added a unique energy and spirit to the narrative, not only as part of the sound track but also as part of the plot.

Lilo and Stitch tells the story of a lonely Hawaiian girl who adopts a stranded "dog," which turns out to be an extraterrestrial experiment on the lam from his creators. An outcast herself, Lilo befriends the strange-looking "dog," whom she names Stitch. Lilo tries to teach Stitch to behave by using Elvis Presley and his music as a model for good behavior. Stitch even plays the guitar while costumed in a white jumpsuit to entertain the tourist crowd.

The Elvis songs used in the movie include "Hound Dog," "Heartbreak Hotel," "Devil in Disguise," "Stuck on You," and "Suspicious Minds," plus covers of Presley's "Burning Love" performed by Wynonna Judd and "Can't Help Falling in Love" performed by Swedish pop group A-

Teens. For Elvis fans, there is a scene in which a pink jeep can briefly be seen in the lower left corner of the screen. Elvis drove a similar pink jeep in *Blue Hawaii.*

Happy Feet

Happy Feet (2006) stands out from most contemporary animated movies in the 3-D format. Nicely directed by George Miller with the pacing of a live-action movie, the Oscar-winner features the voices of some of the biggest stars of the era, including Elijah Wood, Brittany Murphy, Hugh Jackman, Nicole Kidman, and Robin Williams, whose comedic talents lend themselves to animation.

The story follows the adventures of a colony of emperor penguins who find their true soul mates by singing their own special heartsongs that express their very being. A young penguin named Mumble cannot sing, but he expresses himself through tap dancing, which complicates life on the iceberg.

One of the strengths of the movie is its celebration of American pop culture. Each penguin sings in a different style of American music, from rap to pop, and Mumble's talent at tap dancing brings back a uniquely American dance style. Renowned tap dancer Savion Glover supplied the dance moves and sounds that were recorded via motion capture and translated to animation.

Of special interest to Elvis fans is Mumble's father, Memphis, voiced by Hugh Jackman. Memphis sings with a deep Southern accent and moves in the style of Elvis Presley in order to woo his true love, Norma Jean, voiced by Nicole Kidman. Norma Jean speaks in a breathy, high-pitched voice reminiscent of Marilyn Monroe. Clever viewers will recall that Monroe's birth name was Norma Jean. Mumble's parents are incarnations of two of the biggest icons of the 20th-century entertainment industry.

Back to the Sun Years

As Elvis in Walk the Line, *actor Tyler Hilton re-creates a recording session at Sun Studio.*

Great Balls of Fire

Great Balls of Fire (1989) is an interpretive biopic of Jerry Lee Lewis, a rockabilly singer who, like Elvis, had started with the Sun record label in Memphis. In the movie, Lewis is presented as the rock 'n' roller destined to follow in the footsteps of Elvis Presley, who is used as a symbol of the highest level of fame and fortune. To show that this goal is well within Lewis's reach, director Jim McBride depicts a scene between Elvis and Jerry Lee at Sun Studio. Dressed in his army uniform, Elvis finds Jerry Lee tinkering in the studio and bitterly tells him, "Take it, take it all." Unfortunately, however, Lewis refuses to curb his wild antics, which are scandalous to the mainstream public and prevent him from achieving Elvis's level of fame and fortune.

Walk the Line

In 2005, a biopic of Johnny Cash—Sun Records' other legendary son—enjoyed critical acclaim and popular success. *Walk the Line* captures the earliest days of rockabilly, when Cash, Elvis Presley, and Jerry Lee Lewis packed themselves into beat-up cars and drove from gig to gig, where they played to screaming girls in sold-out venues. In this movie, Lewis is portrayed as a holy terror, while Elvis is depicted as the object of unbridled lust for most of the girls in the audience. Together, the pair embody the sexuality and uninhibited spirit of rockabilly—a new sound for a new generation.